Praise for *Never Liked It Anyway*

"A healthy and fun distraction from a messy situation. It's time to move ON with the help of this book." —Bri Emery, DesignLoveFest

"Anyone who is creating anything should read this book, slowly, and savor it, a great way to Bounce back from a breakup or any major life change, even selling your company." —Lizanne Falsetto, founder of thinkThin

"It's time to put down that waterproof mascara! *Never Liked It Anyway* is the one-stop-shop for turning your break-up into the best thing that's ever happened to you. Bitter break-ups are so 2010. Whether you're broken hearted or just looking to reinvigorate your life, who knew moving on could be so fun?" —Taryn Southern, entertainer

Praise for Never Liked It Anyway.com

"Every recently dumped person needs this website." —*Buzzfeed*

"There are plenty of apps and dating sites out there for those looking to fall in love, but what happens when those relationships crash and burn? One entrepreneur aims to help you through your breakups—and make some money along the way." —CNBC

"If you've recently dumped or been dumped and are in need of some emotional and financial support, this site might be just right for you." —Refinery 29

"This is a genius idea." —Adrienne Bailon, singer-songwriter, actress, and cohost of *The Real*

"Why let that tear-stained, boxed-up wedding dress in the garage go to the moths when you can cash in on it? A new start-up site, NeverLikedItAnyway.com, allows the brokenhearted to sell the objects that remain after a split—think wedding gowns, rings, and more—while venting about their exes." —*Huffington Post*

"We all go through it! Why not make the best of it (and maybe earn some dough)?" —*Shape* Magazine

"The site turns online social networks into a potential lifeline. It is the digital version of throwing your ex's stuff onto the street for a profit." —*New York Times*

NEVER LIKED IT

anyway

A Fun and Feisty Guide to Beating the Breakup Blues

ANNABEL ACTON

Skyhorse Publishing

Skyhorse Publishing books may be purchased in bulk at special discounts for sales promotion, corporate gifts, fund-raising, or educational purposes. Special editions can also be created to specifications. For details, contact the Special Sales Department, Skyhorse Publishing, 307 West 36th Street, 11th Floor, New York, NY 10018 or info@skyhorsepublishing.com.

Skyhorse® and Skyhorse Publishing® are registered trademarks of Skyhorse Publishing, Inc.®, a Delaware corporation.

Visit our website at www.skyhorsepublishing.com.

10 9 8 7 6 5 4 3 2 1

Library of Congress Cataloging-in-Publication Data is available on file.

Cover design by Jenny Zemanek

Cover photo credit by iStockphoto

Print ISBN: 978-1-5107-1758-9

Ebook ISBN: 978-1-5107-1756-5

Printed in China

Dedicated to...

Edward Montgomery Erik Luke Eduardo Enrico Bjorn Tomas John Brian Tony Rob Mark Gus Jose Hugh Archer David Kristoph Tom Tim Jack Freddy Sullivan Jackson Wilbur Lawrence Edgar Lake Palmer Nate Roland Adam Lucas Tyson Noah Pablo Carter Mason Ethan Dexter Andrew Jacob Elijah Rupert Mike Salvador Benji Aiden Luke Samson Jamie Caleb Connor Teddy Marty William Stevie Carter Ryan Tommy Matty Atticus Newton Gabe Sven Quincy Henry Paul Daniel Owen Pascal Rufus Nash Gray Dylan Raj Finn Landon Sean Nico Marcus Lennox Wolf Sacha Geoff Wyatt Stan Tanner Nathan Mitchell Alfred Bart Cameron Theon Dom Cyrus Sidney Joshua Ravi Orlando Sebastian Teo Ernie Hunter Brad Sammy Evan Gavin Kirk Christian Max Lysander Raj Otto Anthony Julian John Piers Ronnie Toby Colton Alistair Levi Cole Muhammad Paddy Aaron Tyler Charlie Mitchell Felix Parker Austin Diego Zachary Nolan Lewis Alex Ian Romeo Jonathan Phillipe Christopher Liam Cooper Hudson Miles Rohan Leo Blake Aubrey Mylo Kent Marc Walker Lincoln Jordan Tristan Porter Jason Josiah Xavier Camden Chase Declan Carson Colin Brody Asher Micah Fritz Easton Xander Ryder Nathaniel Elliot Sean Cole Todd Archie Ash Peter Andres Beckett Carlos Flynn Gustav Everett Ryland Kennedy Leo Mack Norbert Oberon Patrick Quentin Raffael Scotty Tariq Spike Trevor Walter Zeke Blaze Jax Zander Ajax Maddox Nixon Orion Caspian Rocco Maximus Ryker Bobby Gordon Cassius Ashton Morgan Fitzgerald Dante Enzo Joaquin Rhett Hendrix Anders Arlo Coleman Demarcus Corbyn Elian Gibson Ignacio Johann Roderick Vaughn Howard Turner Tate Rowan Alec Keaton Graham Gustavo Brice

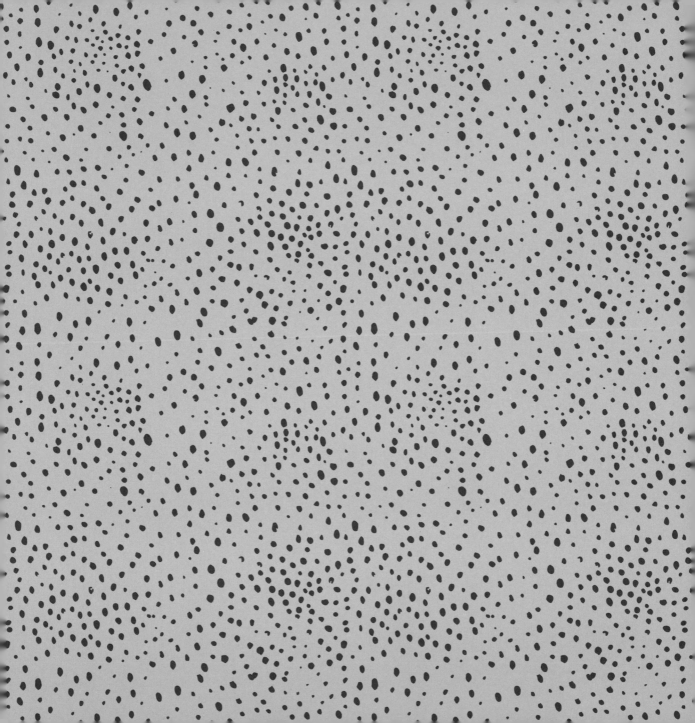

Contents

Shakeup Your Breakup   2

Get Cleansed   9

Get Silly   27

Get Styled   45

Get Creative   63

Get Active   83

Get Exploring   99

Get Connected   113

Get Generous   131

Notes   152

Acknowledgments   158

INTRODUCTION

Shakeup Your Breakup

Dating has evolved like wildfire, with a bunch of apps that make shopping for a partner as easy as shopping for a killer clutch. Yet, bizarrely, the humble breakup has failed to move past pajamas, ice cream, Kleenex, and watching *The Notebook* on loop. Breakups need a massive shakeup. This realization (and a breakup) inspired NeverLikedItAnyway.com—a website where people could offload all their once-loved gifts from once-loved lovers. The idea was simple: sell all the breakup baggage that reminds you of your ex and use the money to buy something that will make you feel wonderful again. Our sellers sell their item, tell their story, share their plan for spending the money they make, and off they go! And it struck a chord. People have sold all sorts of spectacular stuff—from rings to bags to wedding dresses, cars, Harley Davidsons, honeymoon packages, BB guns, a Chewbacca mask—and even a bottle of ketchup.

When people hear about Never Liked It Anyway, they're hit by an uncontrollable urge to share their very own story of splattered hearts and unwanted stuff.

And then they want to know how I came up with this oddball idea. My story went something like this. . . .

A long time ago in New York, my ex and I broke up. There's never really a great time for it, but this one happened a few days before Christmas. A few days before we were meant to fly to London to get merry with his family. I needed to offload my plane ticket and hatch a new plan, fast. I looked into flights back home to Australia, but tickets had the whopping and festive price tag of $4,000. I knew I wasn't $4,000 upset, so I looked to meet friends in Argentina instead. In the midst of my planning fluster, I couldn't help but think that someone else out there was is in the exact same boat—they were probably trying to sell their plane ticket, too. I then realized I had all this beautiful stuff that I just didn't want anymore. It was still perfectly nice, but it felt odd to hang on to. . . . The seed of a very silly idea had been planted.

Weeks later, in a cozy bar in the East Village, I shared the concept for Never Liked It Anyway with friends (and martinis). Everyone laughed and then spilled

2

stories of their own. One had a Turkish rug she picked up on holiday with her ex and had no idea what to do with it, another had a box of unwanted jewelry from her ex hidden under her bed (unbeknownst to her fiancée), and another had a bass guitar she bought and played once after she and her ex had the pipe dream of starting a band. It seems breakups, and their collateral, are a universal thing.

Though it started as a website, Never Liked It Anyway is really an attitude. It's about bouncing back from adversity and committing to being the best version of you—and this book is here to help you do just that. Moving on should be about taking action, and taking it fast. It's about throwing yourself back out there, back into the deep end, and shaking off that breakup funk; because action quiets the mind and propels you forward (and let's face it—your mind probably needs quieting right now). Over the next eight chapters, you'll find a collection of quick and quirky challenges and pointless trivia to lose yourself in. Some of the challenges are simple, others are a little more complex, and all are designed to help you shake things up and step outside your default patterns. Here are some tips to help you on your way.

Better Together.

Most things are better shared. Get your friends involved and make it a party. Think of it is a chance to make your most amazing relationships even stronger.

No Excuses.

You may want to just flick through the challenges without actually doing anything, but action is what makes the difference. Commit to a challenge every day, every week, or every fortnight and make it happen.

Go with Your Gut.

Some challenges will excite you and catapult you into action immediately. Go with it! This is your chance to reignite some dormant passions and talents.

Stretch Yourself.

Equally, some challenges will make you squirm. This is a good thing. Change happens when you abandon your comfort zone and the regular.

Above all, remember this is YOUR breakup wreck-it journal. It's yours to play with, trash, love, abuse, exploit, and most importantly, *enjoy*. So here we go, onward and upward!

Let's Start With Some Good News: Breakups Hurt for a Reason

Breakups are crushing, and there's evidence to back it up. When we fall in love, our bodies ooze the wonder chemicals dopamine, adrenaline, and norepinephrine. Dopamine is especially delicious—it's the one that makes you feel all floaty and fabulous. Unsurprisingly, these chemicals are addictive; love really is a drug. When you go through a breakup, your levels of dopamine go down, and your levels of the stress hormone, cortisol, go up.[1] Research has found that the part of the brain active during a breakup is the same part associated with motivation, reward, and, you guessed it, addiction cravings. In fact, MRI scans have shown similarities between heartache and cocaine cravings. So don't beat yourself up about how your heart is faring. It would be a little weird if you felt nothing at all.

More Good News: This Happens to Everyone

Heartbreak doesn't discriminate. It's oddly comforting to know that you're not the only person who's had their heart broken—it's as universal at gets. These stories come straight from our little site . . .

"We were in therapy for three years and no matter what we tried, we couldn't make it work." Lionel

"He moved to Brooklyn. I'm a Manhattan girl!" Joy

"I want children, she doesn't. What else can I say?" Paul

"His family hated me, and he chose to put them first." Patricia

"We just grew apart. I wish I could hate him. Instead it just hurts." Steph

"We've never been single at the same time." Jonas

"I thought I didn't care that she has been divorced. But I do." Franco

"We both know we're too young, but it still hurts." Maria

"I don't know what he wants. Neither does he." Ariel

"He wanted me to get rid of my cats and I just can't do that." Brit

"Something changed. Why does that have to happen?" Elloise

"He wants to change (and promises me he will) but it never seems to happen." Lucy

"Found out he was cheating in the phone bill. Later found out she was twenty-nine years younger with a drug problem." Jessie

"Broke up with me because his mom said he couldn't marry me . . . after four years!" Lauren

"After six years, one day after my birthday party, that HE PLANNED, he said, 'I don't know what I want.'" Lisa

"He changed the lock before I could get all my stuff from our apartment." Tara

"Straight up told me to eat less when I felt self-conscious about my weight." Brian

"He left me for a thirty-five-year-old version of his mother." Amelia

"He still calls me saying how much his life sucks because he has no money and I'm not there, in that order." Prince

"Broke up with me via text for his ex." Jose

"My guy friend of three years asked me out and a week after we had sex. He never talked to me again." Skye

"My boyfriend of five years lied to me about his education status." Kristi

"He cheated on me while I was pregnant, then got married to someone else." Zoe

"Married with three kids and a dog. Been a proud navy sub wife for over a decade. Christmas afternoon, he told me to GET OUT." Casey

"I cant even explain it. The sex was just terrible. We weren't compatible at all" Leah

"So yeah, he kinda forgot to tell me he had a wife. SRSLY." Mia

Ready?
Let's Do This!

GET CLEANSED

The items we surround ourselves with reflect our reality. Hanging on to old love souvenirs and mementos from a failed romance anchors you to the past in an unhealthy, unproductive way.

It doesn't mean you have to set fire to everything, but putting things out of sight and out of mind makes the task of moving on monumentally easier.
Studies[2] show that the items you choose to keep around you are items that are more likely to be directly linked to your self-worth. And your self-worth shouldn't be linked to your ex.

Aside from the mental toll of clutter, we just don't need it! We already have far too much stuff. It's hard to picture, but the average home is full to the brim with about 300,000 objects,[3] and each year, a mind-boggling 1.2 trillion dollars is spent on non-essential items.[4] It's hardly surprising that we will spend 153 days hunting for lost items in our lifetime.[5]

Our very first chapter is about cleaning, cleansing, and purging the physical and emotional breakup baggage to help pave the way for the good stuff. Nostalgia is a wonderful thing, but it is also a toxic impulse. In the words of the wonderful Marina Abramovic, "We are used to cleaning the outside house, but the most important house to clean is yourself—your own house—which we never do." So roll your sleeves up, grab your metaphorical broom, and let's get cleaning!

Kooky Cleansing Crazes

When we talk cleansing, one of the first things that comes to mind is cleansing our bodies.
We humans have been doing it for eons, in some very kooky ways. Here are some of the strangest.

1. *The Fletcher*: eat whatever you want, so long as you chew it one hundred times.

2. *The Cabbage Soup*: this 1950s diet du jour involved the same soup, three times a day, seven days a week.

3. *The Sleeping Beauty*: Elvis was a fan of this diet, which required sedating yourself for days on end. After all, dreaming is a calorie-free way to munch.[6]

4. *The Master Cleanse*: no food here, just a solution of lemon water, maple syrup, and cayenne pepper, all day, every day.

5. *The Tapeworm*: yes, it's as disgusting as it sounds. Swallow a parasitic tapeworm and have it eat up your food and calories on your behalf.

6. *The Hallelujah Diet*: started by a reverend in the 1990s, it's all about eating as Adam and Eve did: fruit, vegetables, and some whole grains.

7. *The Luigi Cornaro*: in his 1558 book called The *Art of Living Long*, Luigi shared his secret: 400 grams of food a day, along with 500 grams of wine, naturally.

8. *The Vision*: red and yellow foods are the most appetizing, so this diet forces you to wear blue glasses to make your French fries look so vile, you'll leave them alone.

9. *The Ice Diet*: ingest a liter of ice every day by melting it, not crunching it. The theory is simple: melting ice burns calories.[7]

10. *The Werewolf*: followers must eat according to phases of the moon, starting with a twenty-four-hour fast on the full moon.[8]

Create an Ex-Box

Room by room, drawer by drawer, sweep your house for old love souvenirs, tokens, gifts, or relics and shove them inside a shoe box. Photos, love notes on ticket stubs, the hotel pen from that romantic getaway—it's time to get it gone! Take the box to the garage, bury it in your garden, send it to storage, or pick somewhere cryptic for its final resting place. No matter what, just make sure it's out of the house. For a fiery melodic accompaniment, turn up the Beyoncé, Biggie, or Hendrix and avoid Adele at all costs. Finish things off by writing a farewell note to your ex-box here.

Dear Ex-Box,

Cheers for Tears

While you're doing all this cleansing, there's a strong chance tears are going to flow. And *really* flow. Before you curse your waterworks, take a moment to consider just how cool (and strange, and a little bit gross) tears really are while downing a big glass of water.

TEARS.

They are made up of water, oils, and mucus.[10] Tears are like protection for our eyes. They hang out in them all the time. They get around by blinking. This habitual act spreads the tear all over the eye. Your body creates 1 to 2 milliliters of tears, even when you're not crying.[11] Tears lubricate the eye and flush away junk, but also deliver oxygen and nutrients and expel the bad ones, just like blood.[12] Tears get made by the lacrimal glands (near the corner of your eye).[13] They also travel through ducts to the nasal cavity, which is why crying brings on a runny nose.[14] Each eye can hold up to 7 milliliters of tears, and when that's full—they spill out. Finally, be grateful you're not a baby. They cry about 1 to 3 hours a day.

Revamp Your Wardrobe

We hang on to clothes for all sorts of silly reasons. It was your lucky jacket, it cost a whole paycheck six years ago, it's by your favorite designer, the stain is barely, hardly, not really noticeable, or it's just about to come back in fashion. If you haven't worn it in three months, sell it (on neverlikeditanyway.com, of course) or donate it. If it's tattered, stained or holey, toss it. Remember, a clear mind starts with a clear space. In 1930, American women owned an average of nine outfits, but now the average is thirty. On top of that, we wear 20 percent of the clothes we own 80 percent of the time.[9] Indulge your urge to purge and be inspired by the less-is-more mantra! Enlist a friend to slap you silly when you start fighting for your "favorite" skirt "because you wore it in 2007 when you made out with your crush." Toss it! Make room for the new and fabulous.

Stitches with a Story

Chucking out your clothes doesn't mean chucking out the memories. Take three of your favorite items from the TOSS pile and write three little tales about their adventures. Try it in the first person, just to make the exercise even more obscure.

I'm a

_____

and I

_____

_____

_____

_____

_____

_____

I'm a

_____

and I

_____

_____

_____

_____

_____

_____

I'm a

_____

and I

_____

_____

_____

_____

_____

_____

Do The Meditation Thing

Meditation can be daunting, but it doesn't have to be. All you need is nine minutes . . . nine minutes! You can make room for those 540 seconds. This is a three-part meditation. It's a bit creative, a bit ethereal, and designed to help you purge. First things first: set your timer for three sets of three minutes.

1. Get comfy, close your eyes, and sit in silence for three minutes. Don't worry about clearing your mind; just follow whatever thoughts pop up.

2. Next, write prolifically for three minutes. It doesn't have to be good. It doesn't have to make sense. Just write whatever's in your head.

3. Next, draw prolifically for three minutes. It doesn't matter if you haven't doodled since third grade. Just doodle like you mean it and let the marker do the thinking.

Ommmmmmmmm . . .

1. Sit

2. Write

3. Draw

Raid the Fridge

This is not the "crying into an ice cream tub" kind. And not the "sleepwalk to the fridge in the middle of the night and don't remember it" kind. This is a purge-raid. The kind where you chuck out food that's past its expiration date, food you never eat, and food that makes you feel crappy. Taking order of your fridge (and kitchen cupboards) will help you gain a sense of control over your circumstances and leave you fresh, flavorful, and full of feel-good produce. Take this as an opportunity to whip something up with the ingredients that made the cut. If your fridge raid wiped you out entirely, get to the grocery store and buy new ingredients that you usually wouldn't go for. Be creative, be curious, step outside your normal culinary confines, and get cooking! Give your dish a name, write down the recipe, and invite a friend over to enjoy your delicacy.

Bonus: Before you start your kitchen cull, guess the oldest expiration date you will find.

My dish was

This is how I did it

"Don't cry because it's over, smile because it happened."

Dr. Seuss

Make a Face Mask

There's something deliciously symbolic about cleansing your face. Rather than run off to the beautician for a face mask, open up your pantry and make your own. It's invigorating, it's creative, and once you know how to do it, you can treat yourself to some sweet skin-loving as often as you like (though beauticians will tell you to keep it to once a week). This recipe can be tweaked in a million different ways. Just follow this simple recipe to get going.

Face Mask Recipe

½ mashed banana

2 tablespoons natural yogurt

1 tablespoon coconut oil

1 tablespoon honey

Mix all ingredients together, apply to your face for 15 minutes, and rinse off with warm water.

Pimp My Mask

Once you've got that down, mix things up by adding in some delicious ingredients. Then, write your winning combination here.

- Citrus for brightening
- Berries for vitality and energy
- Acidic fruits like grapefruit
- Pineapple for oily skin
- Avocado and papaya for dry skin
- Oatmeal, rice starch, or cornstarch for thickening and texture
- Florals for scents
- Herbs for relaxation
- Egg yolks to hydrate
- Egg whites to tighten

My winning face mask combo

Host a Clutter Party

Any excuse for a party is a good thing. Invite your closest friends—and all their clutter—to join you for an evening of cathartic clutter cleansing. Think of it as a *Pot Luck, Pot Junk* party! Guests must bring a dish and a box of junk they plan to toss, sell, or donate. As you sip wine and nibble on cheese, swap the stories behind your junk. It's a therapeutic catch-up that is sure to bring out absurdity and nonsense: two very helpful ingredients in fighting the breakup blues.

Keep track of the...

Best thing _____

Weirdest thing _____

Oldest thing _____

Saddest story _____

Funniest story _____

It Could
Be Worse

While you're agonizing over your heavy heart, it can help to think about people, or in this case, animals, that have it way worse than you. Yes, your heart may be hurting, but imagine swapping places with one of these little critters.

Queen Bee - Queen Bees have thousands of males trying to mate with them. That part might sound good, but the situation quickly turns. The poor "lucky" mate's junk breaks off inside the Queen Bee and stays in there, acting like a plug. He dies, and the Queen Bee is now blocked off to other potential mates, with bee junk stuck inside her.

Giraffes - To check whether a female is in heat, a male giraffe taps a female's butt to induce urination. He then takes a sip and discovers whether or not she's up for some loving. Lots to be grateful for here, especially that ladies don't pee every time a guy slaps their butt.

Antechinus - This tiny Australian mammal spends two to three weeks on a sex spree, an exciting concept that he takes a little too far. Over this period, he'll have sex with as many females as possible, in sessions that can last up to fourteen hours. The sex is so prolific and intense that he'll start to disintegrate from the inside out. His blood surges with destructive hormones, his fur falls out, his immune system collapses, and he bleeds internally.[15]

Pandas - The number of times lady pandas feels sexually aroused are very few and far between. This miracle window happens only once a year for a twenty-four to seventy-two-hour time slot. It doesn't get much worse than that.[16]

Squid - Female squids don't even have vaginas. Instead, their eggs get fertilized through the act of sperm casting. This sounds as bad as you'd imagine. The male squids use one of their arms to throw sperm-filled capsules at the lady squid with the aim of getting the sperm into her bloodstream.

Velvet Worms - These little suckers have their genitals on their heads. Enough said.

Praying Mantis - The male praying mantis attracts the ladies by dancing for her. If his dancing styles are effective, he'll get the girl—and then get eaten by the girl. The lady praying mantis will let her lover mount her, then rip off his head and eat his body while he's still going for it. Ouch.

Snails - On the topic of ouch, the big act for snails involves shooting sharp sperm darts at females.[17]

Kangaroos - Kangaroos have three vaginas and two uteruses. Which means it's possible for a lady kangaroo to spend her whole life pregnant.[18]

Jumping Spiders - These wiry guys have to put on an impressive courtship dance to win the affection of their lady. And the stakes couldn't be higher. Not only do they run the risk of rejection, they run the risk of being eaten if she's dissatisfied with the do.

Argentinian Lake Duck - These little ducks look harmless at a tiny seventeen inches, but the male's appendage is also seventeen inches. While this might sound impressive, imagine meeting a penis the size of your whole being. Worse still, if the lady duck tries to get away, her lover will lasso her with his whopper.

Bed Bugs - You know it's bad when your mating style is branded "traumatic insemination." The male bed bug will pierce his mate's abdomen with his arrow-like penis. He'll then shoot sperm inside her that travels through her body to find her ovaries.

GET SILLY

Silliness is a stepping-stone to laughter. And laughter is one of the most powerful and underrated healing agents around.

It releases endorphins (a.k.a. happy hormones),[19] lowers stress hormones,[20] relieves stress and tension in your body,[21] and boosts the immune system.[22] And it's a great workout too: laughing for fifteen solid minutes burns around forty calories.[23] In fact, gelotology is a whole field of science dedicated to laughter and its effects on the body.

While it might be too soon to laugh at your breakup, it's certainly not too soon to laugh. Getting your giggle on is a sure sign that things are on the up. For lessons on the art of silliness, we needn't look any further than kids. They laugh like they mean it, play like there's no tomorrow, embrace silliness from the inside out, and laugh on average three times more than adults every day.[24] This chapter's all about embracing your inner kid, taking a page out of their book and having no qualms about looking, acting, or being silly. It may feel uncomfortable at the start; you might have been subconsciously training the silliness out of you piece by piece, but it's nothing that can't be undone. And as Amy Poehler so wisely says, "There's power in looking silly and not caring what you do."[25]

We laugh around thirteen times a day,[26] so your challenge is to make it fourteen. Gather your friends (we laugh about thirty times more when we're with friends[27]) and get silly.

How to Type Laughter Across the World

English speaking folk say *haha* when we find something funny. But what about other countries? Here's how it's done, just in case you find yourself giggling on the opposite corner of the globe.

Sweden: ASG

These three letters stem from the word *asgarv* which means "intense laughter" in Swedish.

Japan: wwwww

The word *warai* means "laughter" in Japanese, which gets shortened to straight up w. And the more w's, the more merriment.[28]

Iceland: híhíhí

Perhaps the cutest of them all, this is the phonetic spelling of *haha* in Icelandic.

Korea: Kkkkkkk

You'll sometimes see it written as kekekeke,[29] but this is the phonetic spelling of laughter for Koreans.

Brazil: Rsrsrsrs

Riso is the Portuguese word for "laughter," and rsrs is the perfect abbreviation.

France: MDR

This is short for *mort de rire*, which quite literally means "dying of laughter."

Greek: xaxaxaxa

It may look strange, but this is a direct Greek translation of "ha ha."

Thai: 55555

This makes perfect sense once you discover that the number 5 is actually pronounced *ha* in Thai.[30]

Nigeria: LWKMD

This acronym means "laugh wan kill me die." In other words, "I'm dying of laughter."

China: 哈哈

These Mandarin characters are pronounced haha.

Spanish: jajajaja

You may want to say jaja, but the j in Spanish is pronounced like an h.

Host a Fail Festival

We've all made mistakes. Some minor. Some mortifyingly major. The more time that passes, the easier it is to laugh at them. And the more we laugh at our mistakes, the less they own us in the present and have any impact on our future. So rather than sweep your mistakes under the carpet, it's time to own and celebrate them—and what better way than to host a Fail Festival! Invite your friends over, ask them to bring a bottle, and come ready to talk about a slip-up from their past. If you need some inspiration to splash all over your invitation, pull from the gems here.

- The Leaning Tower of Pisa, for taking 177 years to build and only ten to start tilting
- The Titanic, for considering itself unsinkable and skimping on lifeboats
- Decca Records, for turning down the Beatles
- NASA, for losing a Mars Orbiter because half of the measurements were metric, and the other half were English
- Twelve publishing houses, for turning down J.K. Rowling[31]
- George Bell, for rejecting Sergey Brin and Larry Page's offer to sell Google for $1 million in 1999[32]
- The Dutch, for discovering Australia one hundred years before the British but dismissing it as a useless desert[33]
- The Austrian Army, for accidentally attacking itself in 1788
- Fox Studios, for giving George Lucas all *Star Wars* merchandising rights for just $20,000 in 1977[34]
- Kodak, for sitting on digital camera technology since 1975, but not doing anything with it to protect their film roll sales[35]

Notes from the Fail Festival

The fail story	The lesson

Send Some Balloon Memos

Ever been mesmerized by graffiti? Or read some poetic messages etched on the walls of public bathrooms? Or laughed at a random poster stuck to a tree in the park? Now it's your turn to spread the silly! Buy a pack of balloons and write messages on the bright canvas while they're deflated. Dream up some wacky dares, positive affirmations, logical advice, or utter nonsense. Armed with your packet of personalized balloon memos, start handing them out to your friends or complete strangers with instructions to inflate and read. Making someone's day might just help make yours. To start, jot down ten potential messages here, then pick your top five to make.

_____   _____

_____   _____

_____   _____

_____   _____

A History of Silliness

Laughter and silliness are timeless. Knowing that people all across the world, all throughout history, joked, hoaxed, pranked, and April Fooled their way through is a marvelous and comforting feeling. Here are some of the most outstanding acts of silly.

In 1698, the Tower of London sent out an invitation to London's elite to attend the annual Lion Washing ceremony. It's unclear how many turned up, but needless to say, there was no lion washing.[36] This is the earliest prank on record.

In 1878, on April Fools Day, the *Daily Graphic* announced that Thomas Edison had invented a "Food Creator"—a machine that could create food out of thin air. Not everyone read the entire article, where the joke was revealed and floods of requests for the machine came in.[37]

In 1905, a German newspaper called *Berliner Tageblatt* reported that the US treasury had been robbed of all its gold and silver. The handiwork was attributed to thieves who had dug a tunnel right into the reserves.[38]

In 1962, technical expert Kjell Stensson took to the screen of Sweden's only TV station to announce that all black-and-white TV sets could be made to see color if a pair of ladies' pantyhose were stretched over the screen. Coupled with a demonstration, it tricked the nation.[39]

In 1976, a British Astronomer on BBC radio announced that a highly bizarre phenomenon would occur at 9:47 a.m.; a rare alignment of Pluto and Saturn would temporarily decrease Earth's gravity, and if you jumped at that exact moment, you could feel weightless.[40] More bizarre still, listeners called in to say they had felt the effect.

In 1980, the BBC reported that the hands of the Big Ben were for sale as the clock was going digital. Bids came flying in.[41]

In 1996, Taco Bell announced its purchase of the Liberty Bell. The outcry was huge, with thousands turning up to protest in Taco Bell stores across the country. They announced it was a hoax and swiftly pledged $50,000 to the bell's upkeep.[42]

In 1998, Burger King released a full-page ad in *USA Today* to announce its latest invention, the left-handed burger. All ingredients had been rotated 180 degrees to make it easier to hold for the 10 percent of left-handers out there.[43]

In 2011, Ikea Australia announced its new product, the Hundstul. It was a high chair for dogs, complete with water bowl, food bowl, and a hole in the back for a tail.[44]

Scavenger Hunt

This is the perfect chance to get outside, embrace your inner child, and lose yourself in a challenge. It's time to grab your phone (or digital camera if you feel like kicking it old school) and get snapping, scavenger style! Over ten consecutive days, take a photo of things from the list here. The list gets progressively harder, which means you'll need to get progressively more creative. For example, if you're asked to snap a giant hat, you could shoot a hat illustration on a giant canvas, a hat atop a brass sculpture, a hat featured on an enormous billboard, or even just a big hat on a miniature doll.

Day One
a cat

Day Two
a barista

Day Three
a tennis racquet

Day Four
a pair of ballet shoes

Day Five
ostentatious Hawaiian shirt

Day Six
comedic moustache

Day Seven
a bird's nest

Day Eight
three (separate) shaved heads

Day Nine
an elaborately decorative garnish

Day Ten
dog and owner that look a like

Rewrite the Alphabet

A is for apple, B is for ball, C is for cat. We all know how it goes. It's the version we all know and love, but perhaps it's time for a reinterpretation—with a grown-up slant, of course. Sharpen your pencil and create your own version of the alphabet.

A is for _____

B is for _____

C is for _____

D is for _____

E is for _____

F is for _____

G is for _____

H is for _____

I is for _____

J is for _____

K is for _____

L is for _____

M is for _____

N is for _____

O is for _____

P is for _____

Q is for _____

R is for _____

S is for _____

T is for _____

U is for _____

V is for _____

X is for _____

Y is for _____

Z is for _____

Create an Alter Ego

Alter egos are an artist's best friend. They're a chance to explore, create, discover, and experiment in a pressure-free way. Now's the time to dust off your alter ego (or create one from scratch) and get your shine on! Alter egos may sound a bit kooky, but when you dress the part, you act the part, and when you act the part, you get what you want. For one whole day, dress in a style completely different from yours and rock that persona from sunup till sundown. Zany wigs, foreign accents, flamboyant gesticulations, ostentatious accessories, and dramatic dance moves are all wildly encouraged.

My alter ego is called

They're all about

Find Me an Alter Ego

The Ziggy Stardust

This was perhaps the most iconic of David Bowie's alter egos that carried him through the seventies. The Ziggy is an androgynous, alien-inspired rock god with a penchant for all things extraterrestrial.

Wear: green, gold, and glitter

Act: like you came from outer space

The Borat

This was Sacha Baron Cohen's third alter ego, a Kazakhstani journalist, utterly oblivious to social norms and etiquette, who embarrassed everyone in his wake.

Wear: your Sunday best

Act: with complete disregard for social norms

The Superman

By day, Clark Kent is an average guy with an average job but then he transforms into a superhero ready to take on the world.

Wear: tight lycra and a cape

Act: like you're on a mission to save the world

The Sasha Fierce

Beyonce's dancing, singing, bumping, and grinding alter ego dominates the stage and stops everyone in their tracks. She developed the persona when she wanted to explore her aggressive side.

Wear: gold, gold, gold!

Act: with the drama of a diva and confidence of a gangsta

The Sex Change

For an extreme change, take a leaf out of Lady Gaga's book and switch sexes. Gaga's male alter ego, Jo Calderone, sees her donning jeans and facial hair while clutching her crotch and a pack of cigarettes.

Wear: a beard and baggy clothes

Act: with swagger and a strong stride

"I believe that in life you should always take the serious things lightly and the light things seriously."

Zsa Zsa Gabor

Personalize a Monopoly Board

Resurrect that old Monopoly board that's covered in an inch of dust and hasn't seen any love since the early nineties. It's time to bring it back to life! Lay out the board, go around property by property, and make it your own. Select place names based on where you were, where you are now, and where you want to be. The cheap spaces like Baltic Avenue can reflect the areas of your life that you are moving on from, and the Boardwalk of the board is where you aspire to be in the future. Don't forget to add in all the juicy little details! Change the railroads to names of places you plan to visit in the next ten years, write out your own Chance cards with things you've always wanted to do, and pen your own Community Chest cards with novel ideas to get you more involved in your community. Once you've come up with the place names, create little labels for each property and stick them over the existing board. Then, just like a kid, invite your friends over to play. To start, write down place names from Baltic Avenue to Boardwalk. Feel free to use the board on the next page.

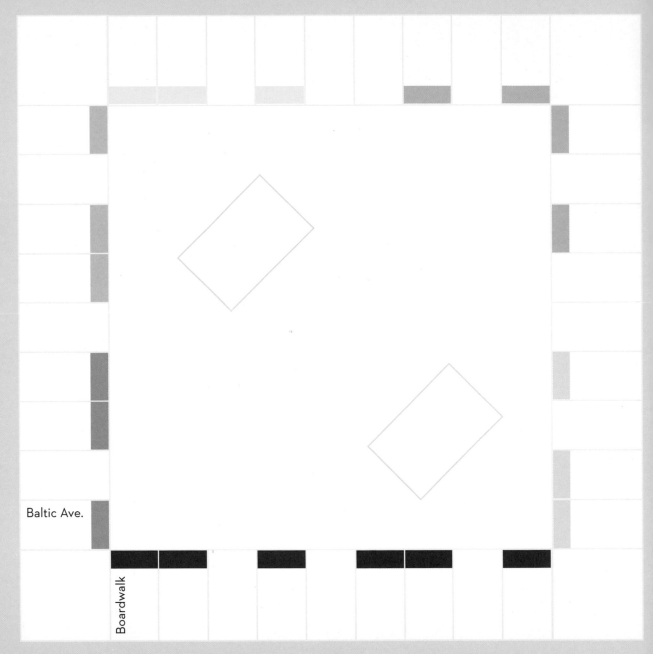

Baltic Ave.

Boardwalk

It Could
Be Worse

You may be nursing a heavy heart, but imagine finding yourself in a classical fairytale. We all grew up idolizing these love stories, but upon closer inspection, this style of loving is borderline creepy. Here's a smattering of some the warped, weird, and wonky morals from our princes and princesses.

1. *Cinderella* – you'll never find love with the wrong shoes

2. *Beauty and the Beast* – there's nothing weird about falling for your captor

3. *Sleeping Beauty* – it's okay to kiss a girl when she's passed out

4. *Snow White* – if you are really pretty, even your own family will hate you for it

5. *Little Mermaid* – abandon who you really are in the pursuit of true love

6. *Rapunzel* – the right guy will fall in love with you because of your hair

7. *Aladdin* – a guy who lies hard and lies often is still worth a chance

8. *Pocahontas* – if you tell a guy you don't want to see him and he replies by grabbing and kissing you, that's fine

9. *Little Red Riding Hood* – if you walk around unaccompanied, you'll need to be rescued

10. *The Princess and the Pea* – you have to be tricked and tested, instead of trusted, to win the love of a man

GET STYLED

It can be hard to talk about revamping your style without sparking some kind of controversy. Of course you are enough as is. Of course you are beautiful. Of course you are uniquely wonderful. But it can be easy to forget—especially post breakup.

There's been a lot of research done into the psychology of how we dress and how it can impact not only our confidence, but also our performance. For example, women perform worse when they take a math test while wearing a swimsuit than when wearing a sweater.[45]

This chapter's all about reenergizing your look, supercharging your confidence, and firing up your magnetism. And just to be clear, we are talking *style* here. Not fashion. Not fads. Not trends. But style. It's always in vogue. It makes the world take notice and speaks volumes without you having to say a word. And most importantly, done right, it's the truest expression of who you are. This is your chance to revamp your style and enjoy experimenting, exploring, and pushing the boundaries of your staples. And it goes beyond what you wear. It's also about how you design your home, how you wear accessories, and what things you choose to keep around you.

Surrounding yourself with good design and things you love sends a message to you that you respect and value yourself. And everyone around you will pick up on that message, too. Coco Chanel once said, "A women who doesn't wear perfume has no future." It's a harsh way of putting it, but she makes a fair point.

Fill in the Blanks

There have been a lot of wise (and preposterous) things said about style.
Fill in the blanks to complete these utterings of brilliance.

1.   Fashion is instant _____. **—Miuccia Prada**

2.   I can't _____ in flats. **—Victoria Beckham**

3.   _____ is the ultimate sophistication. **—Leonardo da Vinci**

4.   Style is _____who you are, what you want to say, and not giving a damn. **—Orson Welles**

5.   Fashion should be a form of escapism, and not a form of _____. **—Alexander McQueen**

6.   Walk like you have three _____ walking behind you. **—Oscar de la Renta**

7.   Anyone can get dressed up and glamorous, but it is how people dress in their days off that are the most _____. **—Alexander Wang**

8.   If you can't be better than your competition, just _____better. **—Anna Wintour**

9.   _____ is the only beauty that never fades. **—Audrey Hepburn**

10.   _____ fade, style is eternal. **—Yves Saint Laurent**

11.   Give a girl the right _____ and she can conquer the world. **—Marilyn Monroe**

Discover Your Signature Color

What is life without color? We see about 10 million of them (16.8 million on a computer screen) and they have the power to influence moods, energy, and actions. This is your chance to play with the color wheel—invented by brain box Sir Isaac Newton in 1666[47]—and pump some energy through your life and look.

The first step is to experiment with the full spectrum of color before picking just one to adopt as your signature hue. Colors are everywhere, so there's really no right way to do this, but here are some suggestions.

- Visit the makeup counter at your local department store and get a professional's take on what colors work for you. Your palette has likely changed since your last visit for prom night!

- Find a nail polish color that fills you with energy, dynamism, and exuberance. Steer clear of the usual pinks and reds and opt for something powerful, bold, and bright like neon blue, orange, or purple. It may seem trivial, but looking down at your nails and seeing a brave pop of color will remind you of your spark.

- Head to an art gallery and take note of what colors attract, repel, intrigue, or repulse you. Don't judge, just enjoy your color exploration and commit to trying on a color that you may otherwise overlook.

As you're playing with color, take note of how the different colors make you feel. Then, when you've explored the rainbow as best you can, pick a signature color and find ways to add that into your every day. From a scarf, to a mug, to a kitchen sponge, adding splashes of your favorite color in unexpected places will improve your outlook.

Rainbow Reflections

Color is a wonderful thing. Jot down what these colors make you think about and how they make you feel.

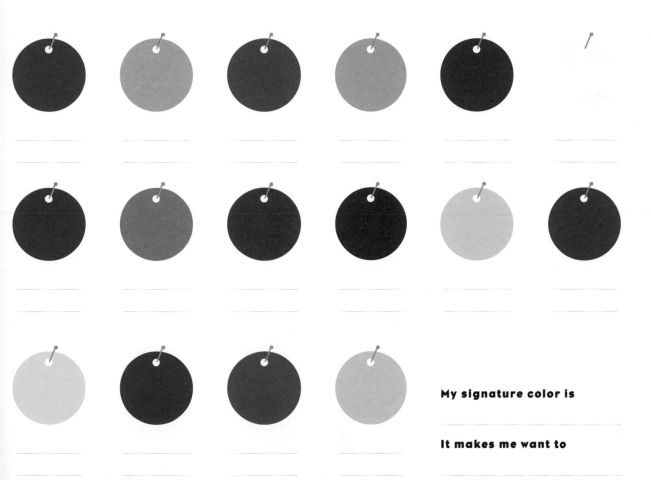

My signature color is

It makes me want to

Stock Up On Snazzy Sunglasses

Take a page out of Elton John's book and start amassing sunglasses. You don't need to take it quite as far as Elton—in 2010, he had 250,000 pairs[46]—but some new shades are a cheap ticket to experimenting with your look. It doesn't have to be an expensive pursuit—just head to a flea market, a thrift store, or even a costume store and pick up the glasses that make a statement and completely warp your identity. Go for the star-shaped lenses, hot pink arms, gold chunks, an old-school sunglass chain. If they feel familiar, set aside that pair and go for another. Grab at least three pairs, and make sure they all make you feel like a different person when you try them on.

Build a Terrarium

Terrariums are so hot right now. What could be better than a little glass shape filled with an intricate world of greenery? Nothing. Unless you make that terrarium yourself. Not only are they simple to make, but they're also simple to care for. All they need it a little direct sunlight, a splash of water now and then, and the odd compliment (for the superstitious among you). You can buy a range of beautiful glass shapes at stores, but you can also use your imagination and repurpose an old coffee pot, jar, or wine glass. Whatever it is, just make sure it's lidless. Now, it's time to build!

1. Clean your glass terrarium.

2. Add pebbles and small stones first (for drainage).

3. Add a sprinkle of sand to fill in the pebbles.

4. Add a thin layer of charcoal and a thick one of soil. All together, these three layers should take up about one third of the terrarium.

5. Plant your succulents and cacti (ask your garden store for recommendations) and make sure their roots bury into the soil. Fill any gaps with moss.

6. This is an entirely optional but fun twist: add old Lego pieces to create an action scene. You might even follow the *Jurassic Park* vibe and add a miniature dinosaur or two.

7. Water your terrarium every one to two weeks. Keep it damp; not soaking wet, not bone dry.

What Would Audrey Do?

Arguably the most iconic and stylish woman of all time, Audrey Hepburn was much more than a pretty face. In fact, what really set Audrey apart was not just her style, but the fact that she had oodles of substance, determination, and guts to back it up. This killer combination has helped cement her iconic status and may even be the reason she has three varieties of flowers named after her!

Hepburn was accomplished to say the least. She won an Emmy, Grammy, Tony, and an Oscar and could also speak English, Dutch, Spanish, French, and Italian.[48] But perhaps her most remarkable trait was her warrior spirit and ability to overcome adversity. Hepburn was just ten years old when World War II broke out and she moved with her Dutch mother to the safety of Holland. Yet all too soon, the Nazis invaded. By this point, Hepburn was already besotted by ballet and threw herself into dance as a way to escape. As she put it, "I wanted to dance more than I feared the Germans."[49] She put her feet to good use and performed in "black performances" to help raise money for the Dutch resistance movement. On top of this, she even helped them by carrying secret messages in her ballet slippers. At sixteen, she volunteered as a nurse for a Dutch hospital that was packed full of injured Allied soldiers (one of whom would direct her in *Wait Until Dark* twenty years later). Defying the odds and helping others became her defining trait. Later in her career, she donated all her on-screen earnings to UNICEF and became a goodwill ambassador in 1988.

Hepburn never considered herself beautiful and dismissed any "style icon" labeling. She said, "I never think of myself as an icon. What is in other people's minds is not in my mind. I just do my thing."[50] And doing your thing is exactly what style is all about. Here's what Hepburn's style is all about. Do her proud and add your own twist.

1 ▼ Eyebrows should be thick and juicy

2 ▼ Sometimes a little black dress is all you need

3 ▼ Flaunt your figure and make belts your best friend

4 ▼ Style should be effortless

5 ▼ Respect the art of color blocking

6 ▼ Stand out with strong patterns and prints

7 ▼ Sunglasses, hats, gloves, and scarves can make any outfit

8 ▼ Keep it classy, less is more

9 ▼ Bow ties, shirts, cropped hair, and loafers aren't just for men

10 ▼ Dramatic red lips are never a bad idea

11 ▼ Tiaras and crowns aren't just for princesses

12 ▼ Pearls over diamonds

Feel the Flower Power

My Flower Powers...

Flowers have powers. Trimming, cutting, and arranging them will infuse some of that magic into you. Head to your local flower market and buy a bunch of seasonal spectaculars and spend the afternoon arranging them into stunning bouquets. To complete the challenge in ultimate grace, grab a bicycle, pop the bouquets in your basket, and ride around delivering them to your friends. When you're at the florist, learn some floral facts about your favorite bloomers; it's all too easy to take that beauty for granted. Sketch or snap a picture of your creations and stick them here.

Decoding Flowers

Flowers have hidden meanings. An enlightening and absurd conversation with a professional florist helped me shed some light on the hidden petal memo. Get ready to decode your next bunch!

Anenomes - "When Will I See You Again?"

The black center is a little edgy and serious, but the vibrant petal colors add personality and show that you're unique, interesting, and a cut above the rest. These bloomers say you're interested, enjoying the flirty fun stage, and ready for that next date.

Peonies - "I Just Can't Get Enough"

These little guys come in tight little balls and over time expand into big beautiful layers of color and complexity. Peonies are a way of showing your depth, and a way to say that you're ready to learn more about your partner.

Rannauculus - "Be My Number 2"

Fondly dubbed "Redunculous," these flirty blooms may be short in stature, but they know how to pack a punch. The colors are bright, the petals are stacked, and they look like a big bunch of fun. These flowers often get sent to mistresses; they're the perfect booty call flower.

Amaryllis - "Don't You Want Me?"

You know things aren't going so well when you get a bunch of amaryllis. These are borderline funeral flowers. Your soon-to-be ex has already mourned the relationship and has found the flowers to let you know about it. This is the "game over" of the flower world.

Gloriosa - "Let's Get It On"

These sexy flowers have sweet and seductive petals that resemble certain body parts. The long-legged stems come in a range of sexy colors. Think red, hot pink, and anything else you might see in a boudoir. If you're receiving these, you're probably getting it pretty good. And pretty regularly.

Restyle Your Bedroom

Your bedroom is the first and last thing you see each day—and the perfect place to start a home makeover. Shake up your style and splurge on those bold pieces you've always wanted to try. Even something as simple as changing up your bed sheets will help transform your space and give it a new vibe. To get ideas flowing, mix and match from the lists below and imagine how a little spontaneity and creativity might create a whole new look for your bedroom.

The Look

Spots and dots

Bright block colors

Mismatched prints

Jungle colors

Gold, gold, gold!

Sexy reds and stroke-able fabrics

Chevron and stripes

Retro prints

Animal prints

Elegant neutrals

Antique chic

The Thing

Bedsheets

Throws

Bed headboard

Lamps

Accessories

Cushions

Wallpaper

Dresser and vanity

Photo frames

Chair

Artwork

"Well-behaved women seldom make history."

Laurel Thatcher Ulrich

Go Antiquing

Head out of town to a giant flea market or antique fair and hunt down some gems. Go all out and don a floral dress, pour a cup of tea, butter a scone, and turn up the classical music in preparation for your adventure. Once you're at the fair, uncover every nook and cranny, burrow in every basket, turn over every trunk, and clamber through the closets with ruthless resolve. Discover the story behind the items by striking up as many conversations with store owners as you can. You just never know what coincidences, oddities, and adventures might unravel.

The item

The story

That Was Worth What?

Not only will antiquing provide an excellent adventure, but you may even uncover an insanely valuable gem. These lucky people turned out to have some gob-smackingly valuable things lying around their home and got that lottery-wining feeling when they finally got them appraised.[51] You may be one of the lucky few to nab a bargain on your antique adventure and only discover its true worth years later.

It looked like...	It turned out to be...	Valued at...
Freaky bone-cups	Chinese cups carved from a rhinoceros's horns in the eighteenth century	$1.5 Million
A dusty old canvas	A 1904 Diego Rivera original	$1 Million
A moth-eaten set of old cards	A set of signed cards from the 1870s Boston Red Stockings team	$1 Million
An old wool blanket	A rare mid-century hand-woven blanket	$500,000
A retro baby's mobile	An original mobile designed by none other than Alex Calder, the inventor of the mobile	$1 Million
A set of mismatched carvings	Four eighteenth-century Chinese carved celadon jade pieces	$1.07 Million
A sweet old lady's brooch	A coveted and rare Victorian piece featured in a sketch by the famous painter and architect William Bruges	$18,500
A teenager's old comic collection	A comprehensive *Peanuts* collection by Charles M. Schulz	$450,000
A beat-up old table	A rare eighteenth-century card table	$250,000
A piece of granny's finest china	A twenty-two-inch plate made by the Prussian East India Company for Frederick II in 1750	$185,000

It Could Be Worse

Romantic comedies or "rom-coms" are one of the most prolific movie genres out there. Invariably, they show our beloved protagonist waddling through a nasty breakup at some point. And invariably, that scene includes a killer breakup line so harsh, you'll be glad it didn't happen to you.

The Movie: *Annie Hall*
The Line: "A relationship, I think, is like a shark. You know? It has to constantly move forward or it dies. And I think what we got on our hands is a dead shark." Alvy Singer (Woody Allen)

The Movie: *The Wedding Singer*
The Line: "Hey, psycho, we're not gonna discuss this, okay? It's over. Please get out of my Van Halen T-shirt before you jinx the band and they break up." Robbie Hart (Adam Sandler)

The Movie: *Superstar*
The Line: "I made up a new dance. It's called the Move On with Your Life." Sky Corrigan (Will Ferrell)

The Movie: *Legally Blonde*
The Line: "If I want to be a senator, I need to marry a Jackie, not a Marilyn." Warner Huntington III (Matthew Davis)

The Movie: *Begin Again*
The Line: "Maybe it'll go away. Maybe it'll fade. But I have to see it through." Dave Kohl (Adam Levine)

The Movie: *Bridget Jones's Diary*
The Line: "If staying here means working within ten yards of you, frankly, I'd rather have a job wiping Saddam Hussein's arse." Bridget Jones (Renee Zellweger)

The Movie: *The Hangover*
The Line: "You . . . you're a bad person. Like, all the way through to your core." Dr. Stu Parker (Ed Helms)

The Movie: *Gone with the Wind*
The Line: "Frankly, my dear, I don't give a damn." Rhett Butler (Clark Gable)

The Movie: *Eternal Sunshine of a Spotless Mind*
The Line: "I should've left you at the flea market." Clementine Kruczynski (Kate Winslet)

The Movie: *The Social Network*
The Line: "You're going to go through life thinking that girls don't like you because you're a nerd. And I want you to know, from the bottom of my heart, that that won't be true. It'll be because you're an a**hole." Erica Albright (Rooney Mara)

The Movie: *Forgetting Sarah Marshall*
The Line: "Peter, as you know, I love you very much . . ." Sarah Marshall (Kristen Bell)

GET CREATIVE

Free yourself from constraints, confines, and rules and take some time to rekindle and reignite your imagination.

Did you know, when you were five years old, you were using 80 percent of your creative potential? Take yourself back to the playground and remember the time when you were in a nonstop frenzy of creating, inventing, making, and dreaming. It felt good, didn't it? Sadly, by the time you were twelve, that number had shrunk to a depressing 5 percent.[52] Not only is it sad, but it's also detrimental to our overall health and happiness. There's a ton of evidence to support the link between creativity and mental wellness. Creativity can lower stress, improve immunity, and even lessen the effect of depression. Not to mention, the power of making things with our hands gives us a sense of control over our surroundings (which is especially good if everything around us feels like it's falling apart).

It's time to get back in touch with your imagination and tinker your way to creative liberation and joy. This chapter will help you find your flow and get in that glorious state of creativity where you don't even notice when it's time to eat or sleep or what time it is at all.

Riddle Me This

Enough talk, let's play!
Match the quote with its maker.

1. "Every child is an artist; the problem is staying an artist when you grow up."

2. "Have no fear of perfection, you'll never reach it."

3. "Think left and think right and think low and think high. Oh, the thinks you can think up if only you try."

4. "No one looks stupid when they're having fun."

5. "Creativity comes from a conflict of ideas."

6. "Creativity is intelligence having fun."

7. "Luxury is nice, but creativity is nicer."

8. "The only time I feel alive is when I'm painting."

9. "Creativity is just connecting things."

10. "You can't use creativity up. The more you use, the more you have."

Lena Dunham

Amy Poehler

Pablo Picasso

Steve Jobs

Maya Angelou

Donatella Versace

Vincent Van Gogh

Salvador Dali

Dr. Seuss

Albert Einstein

Take a Pottery Class

Clay is like mud for grown-ups. In other words, it's amazing. On top of that, there's a lot to be said for making things with your hands. It's calming, mesmerizing, and the sense of accomplishment that ensues is unbeatable. It will require all your focus as you mold, shape, and style the goopy goodness into your very own creations—and watching how you transform a lump of clay into a beautiful bowl will remind yourself that you can move mountains. If you have no time for pottery, start molding some Play-Doh. You can even make your own batch; the recipe is simple, just find it online.

Sketch in the Dark

Sharpen those pencils, it's time to sketch! This might seem like a daunting task, but when you add some adventure, your hesitation quickly subsides and your dormant Pollock splutters out. Go to a place or pick an object that brings you immense joy. If it involves making a little weekend road trip, go for it!

Get some drawing materials (consider charcoal, pencils, crayons, sharpies), whatever you need, and at least two pieces of paper. Now it's time to sketch! On your first attempt, shut your eyes and sketch in the dark. Most likely, it will look terrible and like a series of discombobulated squiggles (though it may look like a new genre coined by a twisted genius. Go you!). No matter what, your sketch-in-the-dark will make you laugh. And once you start laughing, you'll loosen up and get ready to sketch for real. When you feel this creative shift happen, sketch again—this time with your eyes open.

Write the Sequel to Your Favorite Movie

There's no need to watch it again—you already know it line-for-line and can deliver it with enviable flair! Grab a pen and paper and write what happens next in your very own original sequel. Start with the synopsis, and if you can't stop your inner Tarantino, write on. This is the day to unleash your penned prowess!

Here are some ideas to get you going.

- Harry and Sally are expecting triplets . . .
- Thelma and Louise land safely in a ditch . . .
- Rhett Butler decides he does in fact give a damn . . .
- Darth Vader falls in love . . .
- Prince Charming comes out of the closet . . .
- The Godfather sets up a charity . . .
- Bond discovers he can paint . . .
- Jack makes it onto a life raft and survives . . .
- Dorothy returns from Oz and finds herself in Moscow, not Kansas . . .
- Gladiator Maximus survives and goes on to become Caesar . . .

My Movie Called

Here's What Happens

Speaking of Movies... What Would Elizabeth Taylor Do?

She was the ultimate screen queen of Hollywood's Golden Age and the first actress to be paid over a million dollars for a single role (hell yeah!). On top of this, she might have been the first person to turn the "crazy ex" narrative around into something light-hearted, positive, and a source of inspiration. Perhaps Taylor Swift, Adele, and Joni Mitchell learned all they knew from the effortless ET?

Dame Elizabeth was definitely no stranger to the failed relationship: if you Google her, there's a "more" button next to the spouse section as they don't all fit on one page. With that many failed relationships, she could have become angry, spiteful, and turned her back on the idea of love altogether. Instead of letting her past be an indicator for her future love life, she flipped these love mishaps into something laughable and something to learn from. And with eight marriages and seven husbands under her belt, it seems we have much to learn from her! Elizabeth teaches us to accept what is not in our control, applaud ourselves for what we did well, and then laugh at what was not so great. She put it beautifully when she said, "I'm a survivor—a living example of what people can go through and survive."

Husband Conrad "Nicky" Hilton
(1950–1951)

Elizabeth often boasted about the size of her Hotelier Heir Husband's appendage. She revealed, "He had absolutely the largest penis—wider than a beer can and much longer—I have ever seen." Though not even a large member could save their marriage. The couple called it quits just before their first anniversary.

Husband Michael Wilding
(1952–1957)

This marriage lasted an impressive five years, during which Elizabeth gave birth to two sons. But it wasn't happily ever after this time around, either. Rumor has it that she filed for separation before even telling Wilding. As it happens, she had already met and fallen for future husband number three.

Husband Michael Todd
(1957–1958)

Todd swiftly bestowed a 29.4-carat rock upon fair Elizabeth, and by the time they got married, she was already pregnant with their daughter. Tragically, Todd died in a plane crash less than a year later. Worse still, his private jet was named *Lucky Liz*.

Husband Eddie Fisher
(1959–1964)

Distraught at the loss of Todd, Elizabeth turned to his best friend Eddie Fisher for comfort. She soon fell in love with the singer and, in a flash, he left his wife. Elizabeth sparked a scathing media battle, exacerbated by her constant references to her new husband's large appendage and ability to go all night (yes, another big boy husband!).

Husband Richard Burton
(1964–1974) and (1975–1976)

These two megastars gave new meaning to the definition of a love-hate relationship. Burton upped the jewel stakes that Todd laid down and gave ET a 33.19-carat diamond, and so the turbulent two embarked on the rocky road of love. Over eleven tumultuous years, they married, divorced, remarried, and adopted a daughter.

Husband John Warner
(1976–1982)

After her second divorce from Burton, Elizabeth stepped into the world of politics and married the Republican senator John Warner. Years later, she confessed to being depressed during this period and gained a lot of weight, about which Warner was very unforgiving. He admitted to calling her the rude names Chicken Fat and My Little Heifer.

Husband Larry Fortensky
(1991–1996)

After an uncharacteristic decade where Elizabeth took a hiatus from marriage, she married her final husband Larry Fortensky in 1991. He was twenty years younger than her, was a construction worker, and had a mullet to rival Billy Ray Cyrus. They got married at Michal Jackson's Neverland, sold the photos for a small fortune, and then donated that fortune to an AIDS charity.

Get Crafty

It's time to become a weekend warrior! Pick up an old hobby, perfect it, and sell it online. You'll be so preoccupied with honing your handiwork you'll forget all about your heavy heart—and might even launch a whole new career (thank you Pinterest and Etsy). If you don't know what to make, just remember the hardest part is getting started. Start small with the stuff you have lying around your house before you commit to buying new equipment. And use the diagram to figure out where to channel your brilliance.

sewing

Cut up clothes you no longer wear and design something new!

jewelry

Restring old necklaces you no longer wear—use twine as a base if needed.

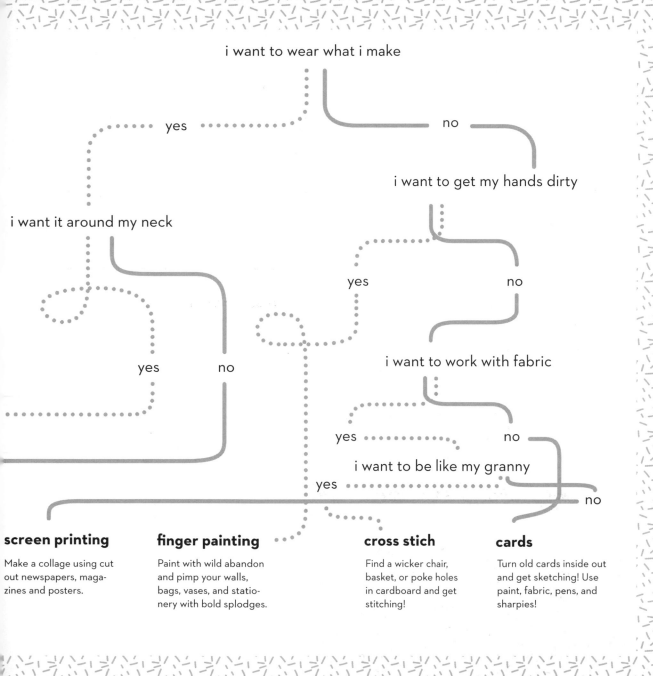

i want to wear what i make

yes · · · · · · · · · · · · · · ·   no

i want to get my hands dirty

i want it around my neck

yes   no

yes   no

i want to work with fabric

yes   no

yes · · · · · · · ·

i want to be like my granny

yes · · · · · · · · · · · · · ·   no

screen printing

Make a collage using cut out newspapers, magazines and posters.

finger painting

Paint with wild abandon and pimp your walls, bags, vases, and stationery with bold splodges.

cross stich

Find a wicker chair, basket, or poke holes in cardboard and get stitching!

cards

Turn old cards inside out and get sketching! Use paint, fabric, pens, and sharpies!

Write a Song

Breakups are an unparalleled source of creative inspiration. Every artist has belted out at least one song of unrequited, doomed, broken, dormant, and disrespected love. Their heartbreak has made its way to the mic and made them millions in the process. Be inspired! Channel your inner Taylor Swift, Sam Smith, or Adele and write about your smashed-up heart. Sing it like you mean it, don't hold back, add in some dance moves, and watch your confidence soar.

My song is called:

_____

It goes like this...

Need Some Inspiration?

Beyoncé – Irreplaceable
Queen B has no problem reminding her men that she's royalty (except Jay Z, it seems). She taught us how to box up our guy's goods, kick them to the curb, and look good while doing it—even with curlers in our hair.
Lyrics to Yell: "Don't you ever for a second get to thinking you're irreplaceable."

Womack & Womack – Teardrops
Don't be fooled by the peppy beats; this little number is the ultimate desolation at the disco. Husband and wife team Cecil and Linda penned the story of a cheater's downfall and kept every club alive from 1988 on.
Lyrics to Yell: "Footsteps on the dance floor, remind me, baby, of you. Teardrops in my eyes."

No Doubt – Ex-Girlfriend
This song beautifully hits on that slow, sad, sinking realization that the relationship was doomed from the start. He wanted to go right whenever you wanted to go left. Deep down you knew better, but here you are all the same.
Lyrics to Yell: "I kinda always knew I'd end up your ex-girlfriend."

Justin Timberlake – Cry Me a River
We've all got one of these. That one person who completely, totally, utterly shattered your heart. They cheated, you found out, you cried. You moved on (finally!). Then as soon as you're over it, they want you back.
Lyrics to Yell: "Your bridges were burned, and now it's your turn to cry, cry me a river."

Joy Division – Love Will Tear Us Apart
The poignant and potent lyrics gave the whole world a glimpse into Ian Curtis's crumbling marriage. The title was an ironic twist on the pop smash hit of the seventies, "Love Will Keep Us Together."
Lyrics to Yell: "Why is the bedroom so cold? You've turned away on your side."

Kelis – Caught Out There
In her introduction, Kelis dedicates this track to all the girls out there who have been lied to by their men. This song encapsulates that red-hot rage that comes when you discover you've got a cheater on your hands.
Lyrics to Yell: "I hate you so much right now."

Carly Simon – You're So Vain
This breakup anthem set the seventies on fire. Simon insists that the song isn't about one vain person; it was actually about three of them. Consider it a multi-purpose breakup jam.
Lyrics to Yell: "I bet you think this song is about you."

Boyz II Men – End of The Road
This is the ultimate heart-jerking breakup jam, if you can overlook the borderline-creepy slow talk in the middle. She may have run off with another fella (a lot), but that's no reason to call it quits (apparently).
Lyrics to Yell: "It's unnatural, you belong to me, I belong to you."

Roxette – It Must Have Been Love
But it's over now. Ouch. This power ballad of the eighties had us all howling in our ripped jeans, flipping our perms, and shaking our bangles.
Lyrics to Yell: "It was all that I wanted, now I'm living without."

Amy Winehouse – Back to Black
This passionately bitter tune comes from a dark, dark place. This particular shade of black is found lurking inside every smashed-up heart across the world, especially when an ex has returned to their former booty.
Lyrics to Yell: "My odds are stacked, I'll go back to black."

Learn Some Mixology Magic

Let's face it: breakups make you want to slam margaritas like they're going out of style. Turn your penchant for Patron into an opportunity to learn all about the mystery of mixology. Invite some friends over and challenge everyone to come up with a signature drink. Insist your guests name their drinks, describe the perfect setting to drink their glorious creations, and what they're raising toasts to. Be sure to have prizes on hand for the winner. Perhaps an excessively massive chalice?

My winning recipe is called

It's best drunk

Here's how you make it

We're toasting to

Boozespiration

A splash from column A, a splash from column B,
and you're a swizzle away from the perfect sip.
Here are some things to try.

liquor 1	liquor 2	mixer 1	mixer 2	method	garnish	glass
Vodka	Berry - Cassis	Sweet - OJ - Pomegranate - Elderflower - Coke - Pineapple - Lemonade - Coconut - Ice Tea - Cranberry - Honey -	Sweet - OJ - Pomegranate - Elderflower - Coke - Pineapple - Lemonade - Coconut - Ice Tea - Cranberry - Honey -	Shake	Umbrella	Martini
Gin	Chocolate - Baileys			Stir	Wedge – Lemon, Lime, Orange	Cocktail
						Champagne
Tequila	Coffee - Kahlua			Pour	Wheel – Lemon, Lime, Orange	Wine
Rye	Nut - Amaretto			Layer	Olives, Pickles & Cocktail Onions	Brandy
						Shot
Scotch	Cream - Advocaat	Sour - Ginger Ale - Ginger Beer - Tonic Water - Lemon Juice - Lime Juice - Grapefruit - Egg White - Tomato Juice	Sour - Ginger Ale - Ginger Beer - Tonic Water - Lemon Juice - Lime Juice - Grapefruit - Egg White - Tomato Juice		Berries + Cherries	Highball
Whisky	Fruit - Curacuo				Grated Nutmeg	Long
					Pineapple Wedge	
Sake	Herbal - Sambuca				Carrot/Celery Stick	
		Flavorless - Water - Soda Water	Flavorless - Water - Soda Water		Sugar	
	Honey - Drambuie				Swizzle Sticks	
	Floral – St Germaine				Cubed/Crushed Ice	

It Could
Be Worse

When you're close to giving up all hope, just remember you could be having bad sex right now. On average, ten million people have sex every hour. That's 166,666 people a minute. Let's be generous for a second and assume that 75 percent of them are having good sex. That still leaves 41,666.5 people having bad sex every minute. Perhaps you need a little refresher. Bad sex is like . . .

Golf – it takes forever and you'd rather be drinking in the club.

Getting a Parking Ticket – you try to get out of it, but once it's underway, there's no escaping. Weeks later you're haunted by reminders, and it stays on your record forever.

A Country Music Song – there's a lot of slurring words and you'd rather listen to nothing.

A Traffic Light – you saw the warning sign to slow down and now you're just sitting there, stuck, and unable to move.

Yoga – it's too hot, you're less fit than you expected, and all you can think about is the end where you get to lie back and breathe.

A Rice Cake – it was never what you wanted, yet here you are. It's bland, dry, and no matter what you add to it, it'll never excite you.

Sunburn – tanning seemed like a good idea at the time, but suddenly you hurt all over and you'd rather not be touched. Anywhere.

Changing a Tire – they said they knew what they were doing yet suddenly it looks like you need to call for assistance.

Mondays – there's a while until it's over and all you can do is think about where you'd rather be.

Going to the Dentist – you lie back in dread, wondering when the power tools and strange noises will stop.

Anchorman 2 – you knew it couldn't live up to the hype, but you went along anyway. Now you're trapped in a dark room, trying to find the exit.

Cotton Candy – it looked so pretty before and now it's just a big, sticky mess.

Oo yea, it's the halfway pop quiz!

You made it halfway! Congratulations. Here's a little quiz about animal hearts just for fun. Get your pen out, then check the answers in the back.

1. How many hearts do octopuses have?
   a.   2
   b.   4
   c.   3

2. True or false? Earthworms don't have hearts.
   a.   True
   b.   False

3. Which living thing can regrow a heart?
   a.   Zebra
   b.   Zebrafish
   c.   Jackal

4. Which animal's heart rate can jump from 120 BPM to 250 BPM in seconds?
   a.   Cheetah
   b.   Horse
   c.   Donkey

5. At 6,000 beats per minute, which living thing's heart beats the quickest?
   a.   Hummingbird
   b.   Mouse
   c.   Dragonfly

6. True or false? Dogs have a larger heart to brain ratio than any other animal.
   a.   True
   b.   False

7. Animals and mammals have four heart chambers. How many do frogs and lizards have?
   a.   1
   b.   2
   c.   3

8. True or false? A python's heart grows bigger at meal times.
   a.   True
   b.   False

9. Which animal has the highest blood pressure of any animal? (280/180)
   a.   Giraffe
   b.   Elephant
   c.   Rhinoceros

10. The blue whale has the heaviest heart of all (weighing in at 1,300 pounds). It's almost as big as:
   a.   A motorbike
   b.   A Mini Cooper
   c.   An SUV

GET ACTIVE

We've all heard about the benefits of exercise, but let's take a moment to marvel at just how powerful this beast is.

It's good for your mind, your mood, and your body. First up, exercise increases endorphins (those delicious little feel-good chemicals we've been reading so much about), and at the same time it lowers the less-delicious stressy hormones like cortisol and adrenaline. [53] In fact, exercise can even curb depression. Studies have shown that cardio activity three times a week leads to a decline in key depression symptoms by up to 47 percent. On top of this, exercise is proven to increase your life span:

people who exercise for fifteen minutes a day have a 14 percent lower mortality risk than those who don't exercise at all. And this is perhaps the best nugget of pro-exercise information yet: those who eat dark chocolate regularly improve their athletic performance by 50 percent! [54]

By now you should be laced up, halfway out the door, piece of dark chocolate in hand, and raring to go. This chapter will help you expand your regular definition of exercise, incorporate some new ways to sweat, and add as much fun as possible. Your endorphins will surge, your anger will dissipate, and even your abs will get a workout from all that aughing. Ready? It's time to sweat it out!

From Stretching to Soul Cycle

For better or worse, exercise has changed a lot over the years. In many cases for the better—especially when you consider the ancient Greeks chose to exercise naked. In fact, the word gymnasium comes from the ancient Greek *gymnos*, which means "place to be naked." Here's a little look at how women's fitness has evolved over the last one hundred years.

1910 – It was all about the gentle stretch. Sweating was seen as unladylike, so they stuck to hip opening lunges in ankle-length getups.

1920 – The stretching continued, this time in silk gowns. Toe-touching was seen as the ticket to fitness, even though dancing the Charleston was clearly better cardio.

1930 – Around this time, clothes got tighter and shapelier, so fitness had to step up, too. Exercises like jumping jacks and leg lifts took over, all in the name of terrific toning!

1940 – The waifs of the 1920s were over, and now it was all about being bodacious, curvy, and busty. Bust-boosting arm exercises were all the rage, along with the "I must improve my bust" mantra!

1950 – This war-free decade was all about the good life, and the hula-hoop arrived to put the fun into fitness.

1960 – Hemlines went up and fat was public enemy number one. The goal was a slim waist and the way to attack fat was side-to-side twisting!

1970 – Jazzercise came along and women kissed the days of passive exercise goodbye. Started by a former Broadway star, this fitness craze was the ultimate cardio-dance combo.

1980 – Next came lycra-loving aerobics, spearheaded by none other than Jane Fonda and her fluorescent leotards.[55]

1990 – Men had been running for decades, and after much fuss in the seventies, women laced up and joined them. By the eighties, marathons, half marathons, and fun runs were the exercise du jour.

2000 – Inspired from the workouts of ballerinas, Pilates took the world by storm with its ab-busting, thigh-crushing ways.

2010 – Hark the glory days of Zumba! The high-paced, energetic, and cultural mish-mash of music and dance styles gripped gyms all across the world.

Now, we have it all! From yoga to Soul Cycle to dawn dance parties, there's a thousand different ways to get your sweat on.

Host a Decathlon

When you're having fun exercising, you don't even feel the burn. Invite some friends over for an afternoon of friendly competition. Task each person with thinking up a sport to play for the day; the more ridiculous the better, like cup stacking, pie throwing, tandem skipping, or yoga-Twister. Buy some borderline-offensive prizes, have some punch on hand, and get the scorecard ready! Like most things, it's better with costumes, so set a theme like eighties aerobics gear, tennis whites, or Hungarian body builder for added hilarity.

My Decathlon Sports...

You Call That a Sport?!

If you're in need of some wacky sport inspiration for your decathlon, check out these oddities from around the world.

Haka Pei
Easter Island, Chile

This former warrior training involves participants strapping themselves to a banana tree stump and flying down a hill often at speeds of fifty miles per hour!

Yak Racing
Tibet

Yaks are not meant for riding, but that doesn't seem to deter Yak Riders entering Yak Races.

Beer Can Regatta
Darwin, Australia

Contestants must make a boat out of beer cans, and then row it to the finish line. Only in Australia.

Buzkashi
Afghanistan

It may look like polo, but instead a wooden ball, players drag a g corpse toward a goal.

Redneck Games
Michigan, US

Toilet seat throwing, dumpster diving, and mud-pit belly flops are some of the events to be found at the Redneck Games.

High Heels Race

Spain

This is LGBT Pride at its best and involves drag queens running a race in heels ten inches high.

Caber Toss

Scotland

This competition requires throwing a nineteen-foot, six inch, 175-pound log to hit a marker while wearing a kilt, naturally.

Bossaball

Spain

This is the Willy Wonka of sports. Imagine playing volleyball atop a trampoline—this is Spanish genius at its best.

Eukonkanto

Finland & Estonia

This is a wife-carrying race and the winner wins his weight in beer.

Sepaktakdrew

Thailand

This is just like volleyball, except you use your feet instead of your hands. Think handstands, cartwheels, and backflips. Easy, right?

Tejo

Colombia

This throwing sport requires tossing metal disks at a ring surrounded by gunpowder. If you hit the target, you'll trigger an explosion.

Learn a Style of Dance That Intimidates You

Whether it's salsa, bhangra, or ballroom, break out those dancing shoes and dip, twist, and funk your way out of your blues. Not only will you get moving, but you'll also meet some coordinated new people, learn some funky new moves, and may even be swept off your feet by a new lover. Remember *Dirty Dancing*? Take a page out of Baby's book and turn up the heat with a sexy dance partner. The time of your life awaits!

Find Me a Dance

You know the drill: close your eyes, move your finger all around the page, then plant it at random and hop to that dance class!

Acrobatic	Gangnam-style	Nutbush	Tango
Break	Hokey-pokey	One-step	Ukrainian
Cha-Cha	Irish jig	Pogo	Vogue
Cumbia	Jitterbug	Polka	Waltz
Disco	Krumping	Quickstep	Xtoles
Electric boogaloo	Lambada	Reggae	YMCA
Flamenco	Mamba	Salsa	Zumba

The move

Learn a Martial Art

Preferably Muay Thai (it's the one with the coolest pants), but jujitsu, boxing, akikdo, and Krav Maga will get the endorphins pumping and the blood running just as swiftly. Channel your energy, find your flow, and kick all that breakup baggage out into the ether. Once you've got some moves under your belt, find some ways to incorporate it into your daily routine; balance on one leg while brushing your teeth, heel-kick your door open, and long sweep your way to the light switch. This is the ultimate in life hacks—exercise, efficiency, and inexplicable enjoyment. Take note of your favorite moves and then make a list of new places to try them out around your home.

The at-home life hack

Run in Shapes

Nothing gets your heart pumping like a good run. But it can be a bit dull. Especially if you're running in circles or, worse still, running on the conveyor belt of ennui (a.k.a. the treadmill). Over the next eight weeks, set off on a little run that maps to a particular shape—like hearts, lips, or waves. Download a running app that uses GPS to track your run so you can see just how good your run-sketch skills really are! While you're on the run, look out for shapes resembling the run-shape you're on—you might find a heart-shaped flower, letterbox, or birds' nest on your heart-shaped run. Not a runner? Just walk it out.

Shape to run

- [ ] Heart
- [ ] Lips
- [ ] Wave
- [ ] Penis
- [ ] Labyrinth
- [ ] Bow Tie
- [ ] Watering Can
- [ ] Stiletto
- [ ] Cocktail Glass

Climb Something

Climbing is really, really good for you. Not only is it an epic workout, it also reduces stress, requires problem solving, encourages endurance and tenacity, and gives you a tremendous sense of accomplishment (and a great place for a selfie) when you've reached the peak. If you want to go big, go for a mountain. It doesn't have to be Everest; just find an approachable yet mammoth one to scale. Pack some energizing snacks, take plenty of water, and make sure you've got buckets of time to soak up the view from the top. When you're that high up, looking that far down, everything feels small—including the blues.

If mountains aren't your thing, find something else to scale. A fence. A roof. A ladder. A tall building. A tree. A wall. A pole. A rock face. A bridge. There are no limits!

I climbed

I saw

I felt

I learned

Get in the Batting Cage

Nothing quite beats the feeling of picking up a bat and whacking an inanimate object with all your might. Head to a batting cage and smack out as many balls as you can. Swing hard, swing often, and give it all you've got. You'll release anger, endorphins, and get a nice reminder of how powerful you really are. After knocking it out of the park, leave your rage on the field and walk away lighter, stronger, and ready for a celebratory Paloma.

If baseball isn't your thing, try other bats (softball, cricket, t-ball), a racquet (tennis, squash, court tennis, ping pong), a stick (golf, hockey, ice hockey, lacrosse), or even your hand (volleyball, handball). Be sure to take note of how you felt pre-smash and post-smash.

Pre-smash I felt

Post-smash I felt

It Could
Be Worse

Band Breakups

Breakups are bad at the best of times, but imagine if on top of your grief you had to deal with hordes of crying, screaming, angry fans cursing your breakup and unsympathetic to any reason you might have for the split. In many ways, these public breakups are much more intense than the straight up "behind closed doors" splits of us common folk.

The Smiths

Lead guitarist Johnny Marr left in 1987 and the band crumbled soon after. He went on to record with a bunch of famous artists and slung occasional insults toward the notoriously egotistical lead singer, including likening him to a mediocre British lounge crooner. Marr said, "I didn't form a group to perform Cilla Black songs."

Oasis

The Gallagher brothers Liam and Noel were famous for their feisty flare-ups, but the inciting incident happened backstage in Paris in 2009. The physical punch-up was more charged than the brothers' normal scraps and ultimately led to their demise. Not only did the show not go on, but the band broke up. A couple of hours post-fight, Noel issued this statement: "With some sadness and great relief . . . I quit Oasis tonight. People will write and say what they like, but I simply could not go on working with Liam a day longer."[60]

The Beatles

Media and fans blamed Yoko Ono for the split, but John Lennon and Paul McCartney put it down to artistic differences. Lennon's first solo album was full of Paul-wrath. The very first song, "How Do You Sleep," includes the biting lyric: "A pretty face may last a year or two but pretty soon they'll see what you can do." What happened to "All You Need Is Love"?

NWA

In 1989, Ice Cube left NWA, insisting he was getting skimped on royalties. The remaining members slapped him about in their next two albums, referring to him as the traitorous American General Benedict Arnold, who flipped sides and joined the British. Ice Cube flung some insults back in his song "No Vaseline," including this gem: "God damn, I'm glad ya'll set it off. Used to be hard, now you're just wet and soft."[59]

Pink Floyd

Roger Waters quit the band in 1983 after fighting with fellow band member David Gilmour over songwriting credits. He then sued his former band mates for continuing to tour as Pink Floyd after his departure. It got ugly, over fax machines, but eased enough to allow the band a reunion tour in 2005.[58]

Guns N' Roses

Just three years in to their rise, Slash had a go at lead singer Axl Rose for his druggy ways, his showing up late ways, and sometimes not at all ways. The band called it quits after their 1987 Use Your Illusion tour and the animosity quickly spiraled. Axl even refused to go to a hall of fame induction because Slash would be there. Fortunately, this story has a happy ending. The band got back together in 2015 for a reunion tour, brokered by bandmate, bassist, and peacekeeper Duff McKagan.[61]

N'Sync, Backstreet Boys, Take That, and New Kids on the Block

The destruction of these four boy bands shattered millions of teeny, tiny tween hearts all across the world. Mark Wahlberg left NKOTB after just three months of swooning, Robbie Williams got booted out of Take That after a drug addiction, Justin Timberlake released his first solo album in 2002 before announcing that he had officially left N'Sync in 2004, and Kevin Richardson left the Backstreet Boys in 2006 to pursue other professional interests.[62] These boy band breakups could be the reason girls have trust issues!

Spice Girls, The Supremes, Destiny's Child, and the Sugababes

But the girls did it, too. Diana Ross left the Supremes to go solo in 1970, the Destiny's Child girls all took on so many side projects that the band was forced to stop making music, Geri Halliwell left the Spice Girls mid-US tour, citing irreconcilable differences and a desire to stop being so "Ginger,"[63] and the Sugababes called in quits in 2011 after thirteen years of subbing their singers in and out.

GET EXPLORING

Exploring is not just about the act of setting off into the wild and seeing what happens. More than anything, it's a state of mind.

It's about indulging curiosity, turning over every leaf, discovering and uncovering originality, delving deep into the delicious detail, and opening doors you've walked by for years, yet somehow never noticed. And it can happen anywhere: in your home, in your neighborhood, your city, or a far-flung destination.

Imagine: what if we didn't explore space? Or the deep oceans? Or what colors look like mashed together? Or what sounds instruments make when played in different ways? Or what can happen when you mix chemicals together? As Stephen Hawking so eloquently put it, "We explore because we are human, and we want to know."[64]

One of the most common traits of all explorers and pioneers is curiosity. And curiosity is a good thing. Studies have found that when our curiosity piques, our brain changes in ways that make it easier to absorb information and form memories.[65] An explorer's mind-set means you need to be comfortable with the uncomfortable. When we venture out into the unknown, we can't have any guarantee on how it will look. Rather than be intimidated by this, it's best to just go with it, let go of any preconceived notions, and enjoy the ride. So get out your notepad, fuel up your curiosity, engage your inquisitiveness, and eat a good breakfast... it's time to explore!

Odd Exploration Game

As you gear up for expeditions of your own, here are some of the quirkiest exploration incidences of all time. But are they true or false? Mark a **T** or **F** next to each.

1. Lake Disappointment in Australia was named by an explorer who was on the desperate hunt for freshwater, but found saltwater instead.[66]

2. Arctic explorer Peter Freuchen hacked his way out of an avalanche with a chisel he fashioned out of his own feces.[67]

3. When Captain Cook first arrived on Hawaiian shores, the natives thought he was their sex god, Lono. Captain Cook went along with it.[68]

4. Chunks of 250,000-year-old mammoth meat were dished up at the 1951 Explorer's Club annual dinner.[69]

5. In 1911, George Murray Levick discovered necrophilia in Antarctic penguins. The findings were deemed so indecent they remained unpublished until 2012.[70]

6. While roaming Hawaii, Scottish explorer David Douglas fell into a pit. A bull fell in soon after and crushed him to death.[71]

7. Greek explorer Pytheas was the first to discover the polar ice caps and propose that the moon caused the tides.[72]

8. To prove humans have an internal biological clock, French Explorer Michael Siffre spent two months buried deep in a glacier, in pitch black.[73]

9. On an expedition to China in the 1600s, British explorers discovered a pickled fish and spices blend called "kê-chiap." Besotted, they brought it home and it later developed into ketchup.[74]

10. English explorer Richard Francis Burton spoke more than forty languages and translated the Kama Sutra into English.[75]

Spend a Day Museuming

Smart people hang out there. Smart is good. Strike up a conversation with one of these smarties and casually ask something like "What do you think the artist did to celebrate once she'd finished this piece?" A serendipitous conversation with a stranger could be just what the doctor ordered. While you're on your exploration, take a little note pad and jot down some of the things that inspire you. Then once you're back home, have a look around your house and see how you might use that creative inspiration to spice up some of your own spaces.

If you think you're not the museuming type, remember that there's a museum for everyone. Some highlights from the "I Can't Believe There's a Museum for That" list include the Torture Museum, Sex Museum, Bunny Museum, Dog Collar Museum, Icelandic Phallological Museum, Museum of Bread Culture, the Museum of Hair, the Momofuku and Instant Ramen Museum, the Museum of Bad Art, and of course, the Sulabah International Museum of Toilets. Whatever you're into, there's a museum with your name on it. Get out there and get inspired. As Italian architect and engineer Renzo Piano put it, "A museum is a place where one should lose one's head."[76]

My Museum Moments

▼ Weirdest thing

▼ What confused me

▼ Funniest thing

▼ What I'll try at home

▼ What moved me

▼ What I want to learn more about

Go Silent

This is a different kind of exploration exercise—one that might push you more than any exerting physical challenge could. Spend a complete day in silence. Pick a day on your weekend, and go about things as normal—pop by your local coffee shop, stroll through the park, try on some shoes, and pick up some groceries. But no talking! You'll be amazed at what happens when you're stripped of verbal communication and are forced to tap into other sources of intelligence, like intuition, eye contact, sign language, and body language. If this sounds easy, ban yourself from staying at home, texting, emailing, and Instagramming, too.

What was easy...

What was hard...

What I learned...

The Worldwide Language of Love

If you keep up your explorer mind-set, it's inevitable that you'll end up on a quest to an exotic new land. And when that happens, you'll need to know how to swoon and be swooned. Try rolling out one of these international love lines when the situation strikes.

Country	Saying	Meaning
South Korea	Wearing beans in your eyes	To be blinded by love
Greece	To bite the metal sheet	To have a crush
China	Dry firewood meets a flame	Instant attraction
France	To be hit by a rake	To be rejected
Italy	Reheat cabbage	To rekindle a romance
Poland	To smell mint toward	To fancy someone
Portugal	To drag a wing	To woo
Germany	To have eaten a monkey	To be crazy about someone
Russia	The tomatoes have faded	The love has gone
Sweden	To fall like a pine tree	Love at first sight
Colombia	Swallowed like a postman's sock	To fall madly in love
India	A piece of the moon	A beautiful person
Brazil	To have seen the green bird	To smile because you are falling in love
Japan	A flower of a high peak	An unobtainable object of desire

Play Letter Roulette

Pick a letter. Write it here, loudly, proudly, and beautifully.

Your task is to have a whole day full of activities, adventures, food, drink, transport, and entertainment that start with that letter. Will it be coffee, comedy, cycling, canyon-ing, and a cheese tasting? Or beer, ballroom dancing, ballooning, and burgers? Now hop to it!

I ate
I drank
I watched
I rode
I saw
I played
I tried

Discover a New Cuisine

Food is one of the greatest discoveries of all time, and fortunately, there's a never-ending supply of cuisines to discover (actually, there are about seventy). Pick a cuisine you know little about and dive in! Learn about its history, main ingredients, serving styles, signature dishes, and any legends attached to those dishes. Find a cooking course to teach you all about the food or go to a restaurant and indulge in its authenticity. If you're really lucky, there may even be a food tour of that particular cuisine in your city. From this list of cuisines here, tick the ones you've already tried, and circle the ones you're curious about or have never even heard of. Then, get to work on trying a recipe at home!

Fusion	*Chinese*	*Mordovian*
Haute	*Islamic*	*Parsi*
Note by	*Circassian*	*Pashtun*
Note	*Crimean*	*Pennsylvania*
Nouvelle	*Tatar*	*Dutch*
Vegan	*French*	*Peranakan*
Vegetarian	*Greek*	*Persian*
Ainu	*Indian*	*Punjabi*
Akan	*Singaporean*	*Rajasthani*
African	*Icelandic*	*Russian*
American	*Inuit*	*Sami*
Arab	*Italian*	*Sindhi*
Armenian	*Jewish*	*Sous Vide*
Assyrian	*Korean*	*Swedish*
Balochi	*Kurdish*	*Tatar*
Berber	*Malayali*	*Turkish*
Buddhist	*Food*	*Yamal*
Bulgarian	*Louisiana*	*Zanzibari*
Cajun	*Creole*	*South Indian*
Caribbean	*Malaysian*	*Yemeni*

Sleep in a New Space

This challenge is open to all sorts of imaginative interpretations, but the intended outcome involves planning a little getaway, with a twist! Rather than plan a normal adventure, plan a trip based on an accommodation style that you've never stayed in. Of course, there's always a trusty old hotel room or a friend's house, but now's the time to embrace the spirit of adventure and push your boundaries. Pick an accommodation option that gets your heart racing and plan an entire trip around that. What about a tryst in a tree house, yurt, or tent? Or an escapade in an igloo, tunnel, or cave? Perhaps you fancy bunking in a caravan, boat, or train? Or a magical night in a castle, mansion, or fortress? Creating a getaway around a novel accommodation choice will automatically get you out of your getaway-as-usual routine and spark your appetite for exploration.

I'm going...

I'm sleeping In...

I'm doing...

Set Off on a Secret Snap Mission

What do you love? Is it hats, typography, clocks, cheetah print, velvet, dogs, books, sculpture, cacti, woodwork, or futuristic gadgets? Whatever it is, pick one particular object and indulge your infatuation by snapping it in a range of different scenarios.

Start by setting off to a part of town you never normally visit. Once you're there, step into every store you stumble upon: bookshops, cafes, galleries, clothing boutiques, antique houses, libraries, variety stores, discount stores, and hardware stores. Track down your object of choice and take a photo of your item each time you see it. Snap aerial shots, close-ups, wide shots, and a bunch of different angles. Play with light, perspective, depth, and framing. And most importantly, have fun with it! Imagine you are a photographer for a new fashion magazine or wildlife journal, or even a movie director doing research in preparation for a film.

Later, when you're back home reviewing your photos, look for a common thread. This may well be the beginning of a new passion project. It was curiosity like this that gave way to entire photography books on doors, floral window baskets, cushions, and porch swings. If you want to take it one step further, create a new Instagram account just for this project. Commit to it every day for two weeks and see what happens.

It Could Be Worse

Divorces are expensive things at the best of times. And when you come to the table with assets up to your eyeballs, it gets very costly, very quickly. Though it might sound like a high-class problem, taking a glimpse at some of these expensive separations might just make you feel better about your breakup.

Michael Jordan & Juanita Jordan – After seventeen years of marriage, the couple split in 2006. Though it was amicable, the divorce settlement took a year to conclude and came in at $168 million.[77]

Donald Trump & Ivana Trump – In 1991, Ivana filed for divorce after she discovered Donald's then-mistress Marla Maples. She confronted her on the ski slopes, got $20 million despite a tight pre-nup, and coined the saying "Don't get mad, get everything."[78]

Arnold Schwarzenegger & Maria Shriver – After twenty-five years of marriage, Arnie's secret came tumbling down: he had a love-child with one of his house staff. The couple had no prenuptial agreement, so under California law, he was obliged to give her half of his $500 to $750 million net worth.[79]

Paul McCartney & Heather Mills – They fell in love in 1999, married soon after, and divorced in 2008. Heather was enraged by her measly $48.6 million settlement and expressed her anger by tipping a jug of water all over Paul's lawyer's head in court. She then spent the entirety of her check in twenty-two months.[81]

Rupert Murdoch & Anna Murdoch Mann – Anna received $1.7 billion after thirty-two years of marriage, including $110 million in cash. Just seventeen days after the papers were signed, Rupert married Wendy Deng, thirty-eight years his junior.[82]

Charlie Sheen & Denise Richards – It may not have been the most expensive, but it was possibly the ugliest (and most public) celebrity divorce of all time, due to a spate of abusive voice messages from Charlie. In a triumphant burst of rage, he called his former wife a "sad, jobless pig who is sad and talentless and sad and jobless and evil and a bad mom" and topped it off by suggesting she "go cry to her bald mom."[83]

Guy Ritchie & Madonna – Ritchie got just $10 million of Madonna's estimated $300 million net worth. He also had to sign a clause that prevented him from ever talking about their seven-year marriage.[84]

Katie Holmes & Tom Cruise – An airtight pre-nup froze Katie out of Tom's $250 million net worth. Instead, she receives $400,000 in child support each year until their daughter, Suri, turns eighteen.[85]

GET CONNECTED

Human connection is paramount. Without it, we shrink, shrivel, and wither. A recent study found that a lack of connection can be even more detrimental to health than smoking, obesity, and high blood pressure.[86]

When we're connected, it not only feels better, but it improves our health. Your immune system gets a boost, inflammation dissipates, stress hormones reduce, and anxiety and depression drop.[87] On top of this, social connection can lengthen your life.[88] In fact, extreme loneliness can increase the chance of early death by 14 percent.[89] And we're not just talking about human connections. People with pets also report lower blood pressure, less stress, and tend to be cheerier, more trusting, and more social.[90]

You might want to hide after a breakup, but getting back out there, being social, and meeting new people (who you have no painful ties with) will help you rediscover your brilliant self. And there's some science to back that up: those who feel connected have higher self-esteem, greater empathy for others, and are more trusting and collaborative. This in turn helps them deepen their relationships and also develop new ones. It's the gift that keeps on giving.

Just to be clear, we're not talking about connecting on Facebook, hearting your way around Instagram, or sharing a Vine; we mean the real stuff. The face to face. The up close and personal. The deep and dirty conversations with your friends. And the random, serendipitous connections with strangers. This is the stuff that matters. Now's the time to leave the comfort of the couch, step outside, and connect in juicy new ways.

Did You Get My Pigeon Post?

Never before has it been so easy to connect. Imagine if you wanted to end a relationship, or start a new one, and you had to orchestrate a pigeon carrier, set off a smoke signal, or run a marathon to get your message through. Let's all take a moment and be grateful for all the ways we can date (and dump) each other today.

33,000 BC – Cave Paintings

Neanderthals used paint to communicate messages inside caves, mainly of what they had seen, heard, and killed that day. Some theories propose that they were warning which foods were safe to eat, though the jury is still out on that one (and likely will be forever).[91]

Limitation: You had to be inside the cave to get the message.

490 BC – Running

After beating the Persian army, the Greeks had a momentary panic that the Persians would make a detour and invade Athens on their way home. So they sent a running messenger, Pheidippides, to run twenty-six miles to Athens to deliver their capital warning.[92] He died soon after the dash.

Limitation: The ability to run twenty-six miles every time you wanted to say something.

484 BC – Relay Road Couriers

The Persians built a 1,777-mile stretch of highway that ran through their empire called the Royal Road. A professional squad of Relay Road Couriers transported secret messages up and back.

The couriers and their horses were dotted along the road at designated stations and would sub in and sub out all the way along. Each courier and horse was responsible for a full day's ride.[93]

Limitation: You had to stick to routes with relay stations.

150 BC – Smoke Signals

The Chinese set off smoke signals to warn of danger along the Great Wall with thick, dense smoke that could be seen up to three hundred miles away[94] The special smoke was made from a mixture of saltpeter, sulfur, and the magic ingredient, wolf dung!

Limitation: This was not like sky-writing airplanes; legible writing was impossible.

1150 AD – Carrier Pigeon

Pigeon post started in the twelfth century and zipped messages from the Pharaohs all the way to Iran, Iraq, and Assyria. They were also used a lot in World Wars I and II as the brave little pigeons could fly high above the battlefields and obstructive smoke.[95]

Limitation: Forget long distance shipping or anything much heavier than a letter.

Make a Mix Tape

Yes, a cassette-mix tape. The old-school ones that melt in the sun, leave their ribbons in a tangled mess, and are impossible to play since cassette players have been on the brink of extinction for decades. If this is too difficult (which is highly likely), turn to the powers of Spotify, SoundCloud, or Tidal and make a digital one. Pick three of your closest friends and think about some of your most epic adventures and relive the soundtrack to accompany it. Once you've built your playlist, don't just email the link to your mates—create an album cover and title, too. Make it silly. Make it ostentatious. Make it personal. Then, send your cover along with a link to the tunes themselves. Your friends will be speechless, and no doubt a big fat catch-up will ensue.

Album Title _____

Song list	For the time when

What's in a Name?

If you need some inspiration, these album titles should steer you in the so-wrong-it's-right direction. You'll notice that most of the funny ones happened in the 1970s and '80s. Perhaps it's time to resurrect some of that bell-bottom, glitter-spangled nonsense.

- REO Speedwagon – You Can Tune a Piano, but You Can't Tuna Fish (1978)
- Caravan – If I Had To Do It All Over Again I'd Do It All Over You (1970)
- George Clinton – Hey Man . . . Smell My Finger (1993)
- Landscape – From the Tea-rooms of Mars . . . to the Hell-holes of Uranus (1981)
- Meat Loaf – Hang Cool Teddy Bear (2010)
- Leo Kottke – My Feet Are Smiling (1973)
- Belle and Sebastian – Fold Your Hands Child, You Walk Like a Peasant (2000)
- David Bromberg – Bandit in a Bathing Suit (1978)
- Paul McCartney – Kisses on the Bottom (2012)
- Spooky Tooth – You Broke My Heart . . . So I Busted Your Jaw (1973)
- The Unicorns – Who Will Cut Our Hair When We're Gone? (2003)
- Amazing Rhythm Aces – How The Hell Do You Spell Rythum? (1980)
- Midnight Star – No Parking on the Dance Floor (1983)
- Southside Johnny & The Jukes – At Least We Got Shoes (1986)
- Sparks – Angst in My Pants (1982)
- Alice Cooper – Zipper Catches Skin (1982)
- The Association – Waterbeds in Trinidad! (1972)[96]

Join a Chorus

Singing is liberating at the best of times and singing as part of a group is even more powerful. You'll be blown away at your ability to connect with people you've just met, and the power of voices when they come together. If the idea of a choir sounds a bit serious, there are plenty of light-hearted sing-alongs in need of your vocal contribution. There are sing-a-long movies, football team anthems, national anthems, university clubs, comedic singing groups, and musical groups that all need a good pair of lungs and might be more up your vocal alley. It doesn't matter how good your voice is; there's strength in numbers. Belt it out. Go for the high notes. Put your back into it. And enjoy the sweet taste of choral freedom.

What I learned when I belted it out...

Love Potions and Aphrodisiacs

You might not feel like connecting with anyone just yet, but if you eat enough aphrodisiacs, your situation might change. Rapidly. Here is some food to get you in the mood.

Chocolate — This sweet treat is packed with the chemicals anandamide and phenylethylamine that boost the happy hormone serotonin.[97] Nibble on the really dark stuff and turn off the lights.

Oysters — As Jonathan Swift said, "He was a bold man that first ate an oyster."[98] Experts believe it's the physicality of oysters—the sucking, slurping, and touching—that turns us on.[99] Though they're also full of zinc, which boosts semen production.

Chilies — These little fiery numbers really do turn up the heat! Chilies get your heart racing, increase blood circulation, and stimulate nerve endings.[100] Just be sure to wash your hands before you reach for your lover.

Truffles — Though there's little science to back it up, truffles are strongly associated with sex. Napoleon ate these "testicles of the earth" as often as he could to increase his potency.[101] Perhaps it's just their rarity and intimidating price tag that make them so alluring.

Watermelon — This juicy pink fruit works the exact same way Viagra does—thanks to a healthy amount of the amino acid citrulline.[102] That third watermelon martini finally makes sense.

Avocados — They may be toxic to horses, but to humans they are just ace.[103] Their rich vitamin E content helps produce hormones, which in turn stimulate sexual responses.[104] And their beautiful womanly shape can't hurt.

Maca — This root from the Andes is most commonly crushed into powder and made into cookies, shakes, and bread. Maca is full of sterol, a chemical that boosts libido and sex drive.[105]

Vanilla — This sweet bean can heighten sexual sensations by stimulating nerves.[106] In case you needed convincing, dessert is always a good idea.

Pomegranates — Dubbed the love apple, these pretty pink numbers are packed full of antioxidants that help protect blood vessel lining, which increases blood flow, which increases sensitivity—in all the right places.[107]

Bring Dog Treats to the Dog Park

Dogs are excellent at finding happiness. They take things as they come and bask wholeheartedly in the small tidbits that make them happy. Think toys, sticks, treats, and affection. We have a lot to learn from our four-legged friends. Head to your local dog park with a pouch of dog treats and meet some fluffy little creatures. To feed someone else's dog, you'll need to strike up a conversation with the owner. Conversing with strangers can be intimidating, but it's a rewarding experience and reminds you that people are just people. And who knows, you might end up with a new friend, or even a date. Challenge yourself to meet at least ten pooches and people, then write about it here.

The Pooch	The Owner	The Chat

Dog Biscuit Recipe

If you really feel like going all out, make the dog biscuits yourself. Here's a simple little recipe.

You'll need:

2½ cups flour

1 cup oats

1 egg

1 bouillon cube

½ cup hot water

a handful of bonus bits (think bacon bits, beef strips, carrots, peas, cheese, peanut butter, apple slices, coconut strips, or pumpkin pieces)

Then you'll have to:

Set the oven to 350 degrees.

Dissolve the stock cube in hot water and add all the ingredients together to form a dough. Then knead it heartily into a ball.

Roll out your dough until it's about ½ inch thick and create little bone shapes with a cookie cutter or a precise knife and rock-steady hand.

Place biscuits on a greased cookie sheet and cook for 30 minutes.

Host a Memory Lane Party

This is a potluck party with a twist. Invite your friends over and ask them to bring a favorite dish that reminds them of their childhood. When your guests arrive, have color markers and note cards handy for people to write about why their dish got lodged in their food memory bank, and plant it right next to their dish. This is the ultimate conversation starter and will get your guests mingling in ways that defy the dreaded "what do you do?" small talk. To really amplify the connection effect, ask everyone you invite to bring a guest—but make it someone they just met that week. Capture some of your friends, winning best dishes, and memories below.

The friend	The dish	The memory

"Make your interactions with people transformational, not just transactional."

— Patti Smith

Get a Date

Truth is, you have to get back out there sooner or later. And it may as well be sooner. This challenge doesn't mean tracking down your perfect mate; it just means being brave enough to put yourself out there and connect with a stranger for a small chunk of time. Try one of the millions of dating apps, or if you're not the online type, head out to one of your favorite places (one you are drawn to because of passion, not necessarily a bar... but bars are pretty good, too). If you're really up for an adventure, or subscribe to the kiss-plenty-of-frogs theory, try your hand at speed dating. And no matter what you're doing or where you are, linger longer, smile more, and chat with strangers. Be open to being approached and doing the approaching, too. Don't forget to tell your friends that you're on the date-hunt. You never know who they might send your way.

Conversation Starters

When conversation dries up, it happens fast. You notice it. They notice it. Then suddenly you're stranded in the Sahara of silence, searching for an oasis of words. The usual weather-and-work chat can wear quite thin, so shake it up with some of these conundrums. Make sure you both answer—there's no room for fence-sitting! And remember, your antidote to the awkwardness of new interactions is to smile, sit up, and lighten up.

Would you rather...

Live in the desert, or the jungle?

Lose your sex organs, or lose your hands?

Become a hermit, or share a bedroom with five people?

Have to wear a bike helmet at night, or a baseball cap every day and every night?

Be disgustingly rich and lose it all, or have a small amount forever?

Be a famous singer, or a famous scientist?

Have three eyes, or no eyes?

Live until you're 40, or live until you're 240?

Have invented the iPhone, or penicillin?

Have a pet spider, or a pet snake?

Go back in time, or go to the future?

Be able to teleport, or see through walls?

Be without Wi-Fi, or have no transport options other than walking?

Eat pigeon roadkill, or squirrel roadkill?

Befriend one lion, or understand all birdsong?

Be able to fly, or swim underwater without coming up for air?

Have no taste buds, or eat the exact same thing every day until you die?

Give Free Advice

You've seen them at parks, beaches, markets, and gardens. Those oddballs with a sign saying FREE ADVICE. Chances are, they're not oddballs at all; they're just regular people taking up a challenge like this! Grab a friend, make a sign (the more neon paint, the better), and head down to your local neighborhood thoroughfare, stick up your sign, and see what comes. You'll meet a full spectrum of characters and hear all sorts of interesting problems—problems that will likely make you forget about your own. As far as challenges go, this is pretty out there, but nothing you can't take on. Pluck up some courage and start dispensing some wisdom.

What I learned that time I made a random sign and dished out advice...

"A woman is like a tea bag—you never know how strong she is until she gets in hot water."

—Eleanor Roosevelt

It Could Be Worse

In the thick of your sorrow, take some time to bask in the good fortune of not having a really oddball sexual fetish, or being with someone who does. And if you do, or they do, to each their own! Here's a list of some of the kookiest.

Dendrophilia – We all love trees, but these people really, really love trees.[108]

Mucopholia – Yes, you spy the word mucus! If you find sneezing inexplicably seductive, you should join these guys.[109]

Avisodomy – Feathers in the bedroom might be commonplace, but this very particular form of bestiality involves actually having sex with birds.[110]

Frotteurism – This one's about touching a stranger in a crowded place and feeling the heat.[111]

Oculolinctus – Eyes are the window to the soul, and some people just love to lick and suck them.[112]

Emetophilia – For most of us, vomiting is the pinnacle of trauma. To others, it's just plain hot.[113]

Formicophilia – This one's all about insect and snail love. Apparently, there's nothing quite like letting them run wild all over your genitals.[114]

Coulrophilia – Who says clowns are terrifying? To some, a clown makes you want to get down.[115]

Kleptolagnia – Kleptomaniacs find stealing thrilling; these guys find it titillating.[116]

Voraphilia – Ever had your lover say they want to eat you up? These guys mean it. They fantasize about being swallowed whole.[117]

Psychrophilia – Some like it hot, others like it cold. This one's all about watching people freeze.[118]

Eproctophilia – In a logic-defying twist, eproctophiles find human flatulence a turn on.[119]

Climacophilia – Love is a dangerous game, especially if you've got this fetish and get off on watching people fall down stairs.[120]

Taphephilia – Astonishingly, to some people, being buried alive is like winning the erotic jackpot.[121]

GET GENEROUS

Generosity is one of the most attractive qualities going around. It's more than just buying stuff for people (though that's a nice thing to do); it's about generosity of spirit, of time, energy, and being unexpectedly thoughtful.

And most importantly, not expecting anything in return. According to some sources, Winston Churchill summed it up beautifully when he said, "We make a living by what we get. We make a life by what we give."[122]

Though it goes against what generosity is all about, being generous is actually good for your health. When we give, the pleasure and reward centers of our brain light up as if we were the one receiving the pretty parcel. [123] Volunteering is particularly powerful. Those who make a habit of giving away their time have lower blood pressure, report less sleeplessness, helplessness, and hopelessness, and form rock-steady friendships.[124]

On top of that, generosity makes our brain release the wonder chemical oxytocin that lowers stress and makes us feel connected to people.[125] It's no surprise that it's the exact same chemical released during sex.

When it comes to generosity, it's not just about being generous to others. It's just as important, if not more so, to cut yourself some slack and be generous and loving to yourself. So dig deep, share, volunteer, donate, and give like you can't give anymore. The more you give, the more you'll trigger a ricochet of positivity in all sorts of weird and wonderful ways.

Give It Away Now!

Each year, the World Giving Index measures generosity across the world. It looks for a combination of things: donating money to a cause, volunteering time to a charity, and helping strangers out. From the list of countries below, which do you think are the most generous? Rank them in order from 1 to 10, with 1 being the most giving.

Canada	Malaysia	United Kingdom	New Zealand	Ireland
Sri Lanka	Myanmar	United States	Netherlands	Australia

1.

2.

3.

4.

5.

6.

7.

8.

9.

10.

Host a Webinar

Over the course of a lifetime, we accumulate tons of knowledge. Some useful, some useless, but for the most part, it's all mightily magnificent in its own way. You may not think you're an expert in anything just yet, but your perspective is yours and yours alone. Let's say you want to teach a design class. You may think you have nothing new to add, but you do. A lot, in fact! Only you can teach a class that incorporates some fascinating lessons you picked up elsewhere. Perhaps it was that technique you picked up from painting with your grandma, or that method you discovered in that cooking class you did in Italy, or some existential theory from your philosophy degree. Those experiences are unique to you. This is your chance to smash together all the lessons you've ever learned along the way and use them to share an exciting point of view. If you throw in some examples and stories to back up your perspective, then you'll have a hot little webinar ready to go!

My class is called
I'll teach
My point of view is
My stories to back it up are

Stumped for Topics?

If you're in need of some inspiration, take a cue from some of these wacky thesis topics.[126] Yes, that's right, people dedicated at least three years of their lives to sleepless study in the name of these gems.

The Unhidden Dangers of Sword Swallowing

Booty Calls: The Best of Both Worlds?

Do Woodpeckers Get Headaches?

Wet Underwear: Not Comfortable

Does Country Music Make You Suicidal?

Ovulation: A Lap Dancer's Secret Weapon

Flatulence as Self-Defense

Even Chickens Prefer Beautiful People

Love and Sex with Robots

The Possibility of Unicorns

A Better Approach to Penile Zipper Entrapment

Fruit Bat Fellatio

Gay Dead Duck Sex

Can Pigeons Tell a Picasso from a Monet?

The Rectal Route to Curing Hiccups

Volunteer in a Soup Kitchen

Giving is good. And when it's in your neighborhood, it's a chance to understand a side that you might otherwise gloss over. Join your local soup kitchen, food drop, or homeless shelter and lend a helping hand. Engage in as many deep, personal, and meaningful conversations as possible. While handing out supplies and food is valuable, it's the respectful and intimate conversations you have with the recipient that will have the most impact—on both of you. Not to mention that hearing some true tales of suffering might put your own woes in perspective.

What struck and stuck with me...

Break Me Off a Piece of That!

One way to be generous is to feed people. And feed them well. Of course, that includes hydrating them, too! Here are some of the biggest, most extravagant, and excessively lavish ingestibles ever made.

 The Largest Cheesecake – This 6,900-pound whopper was made at the ninth annual Cream Cheese Festival in 2013. The cake was 90.25 inches in diameter, 31 inches deep, and served 24,533 people.[127]

 The Longest Sandwich – In a move that makes a foot-long look like an amateur bite, a Lebanese community banded together in 2011 to craft the longest sandwich on record. It was 2,411 feet long, took twenty-two hours to make, and 639 people to fill it! [128]

 The Largest Lasagna – This was a collaborative effort between a Polish restaurant and a local supermarket chain. The lasagna was 82 feet long, 8.2 feet wide, and weighed an incomprehensible 10,725 pounds. [129]

 The Most Expensive Cocktail – This pricey little number came from the masterminds at Gigi's restaurant in London. The cocktail is made of 1990 vintage Cristal and Armagnac from 1888 and sells for $13,367. That's about $90 per milliliter.[131]

 The Most Champagne Bottles Sabered – On the topic of champagne, the most champagne bottles simultaneously sabered happened at an event in Mendrisio, Switzerland. An astounding 487 bottles were knifed open, and in an extra twist of generosity, all the money raised went to charity.[132]

 The Highest Champagne Fountain – Still on the topic of champagne, the largest champagne fountain was assembled in Belgium. It was sixty-three stories high and made with 43,680 glasses.[133]

Give the Gift of Time

It's the one thing we all want more of, but no matter how much money you have spilling out of your seams, you can't buy more. But you can donate it. Lay off the foodie snaps and fashion flat-lays and put Facebook to good use: offer your time to your friends. Someone might need help babysitting, reading their movie script, reviewing their app idea, cleaning out their garage, or returning library books three years overdue. This small gesture on your part will blow your friends away, make you feel splendid all over, and likely inspire you to make a habit of it.

I gave a couple of hours of my time and...

Random Acts of Kindness

While you're helping a friend, help some strangers you meet out and about.

- Fill a parking meter
- Give compliments, and lots of them
- Tell someone how they have changed your life
- Give away things you don't need
- Leave things neater than you found them
- Leave people better than you found them
- Send a postcard
- Give a flower to a stranger
- Tape change to a vending machine
- Feed the birds
- Smile
- Hold a hug just a second longer

- Leave surprise notes for people you care about
- Buy a stranger a cup of coffee
- Give a book away
- Tell someone you're thinking of them
- Cook for someone
- Write a thank-you note
- Give up your seat
- Leave a note for your server
- Read to someone who can't
- Walk a neighbor's dog
- Let someone skip the line
- Ask how you can help

"They always say time changes things, but you actually have to change them yourself."

Andy Warhol

Get Green

Head to your local park, beach, garden, or Main Street and pick up some litter. Remember in Get Cleansed how cleaning up your immediate surroundings can help you regain a sense of control? Luckily, the same is true of cleaning up the big wide world around you. And it needs to happen. Did you know one mile of highway contains about 16,000 pieces of litter? Each year, the US government spends about $11 billion cleaning up the problem.[134] Yuck! Don some gloves, grab a big bag, and bring a device that can blast the melodies. The goal here is to have as much fun as possible, and make it obvious to anyone walking by. We humans are suckers for fun, and have a natural desire to join in the good times. With a little luck, you'll have others wanting to join in your efforts in no time.

Top off your morning of cleaning with a trip to your local community garden and plant a tree, shrub, or flowers for everyone to enjoy. Visit it regularly to make sure it—and its friends—are getting the water, and love, they need.

Write a Love Letter to Yourself, Ransom-Note Style

It's often easier to be generous to others than to yourself. And as Diane Von Furstenberg says, "You're always with yourself, so you might as well enjoy the company."[135]

Sitting down to write yourself a love letter is as cringe-worthy as it gets. Unless it's done ransom-note style! Grab old papers and magazines, cut out your ode to yourself, and stick the letters, psycho-killer style, here. Call out all your best bits and remind yourself why you're special. If it helps, imagine it's someone in your family or a close friend writing about you. That should get you going. Stick your note here.

Famous Love Letters

So they may not have been love letters to themselves or written ransom-note style, but these four handwritten love letters from Jimi Hendrix, Frida Kahlo, Johnny Cash, and Napoleon should give you some inspiration.[136]

```
Little girl . . .
Happiness is within you . . . so unlock the chains from your heart and let
yourself grow- Like the sweet flower you are . . .
I know the answer-just spread your wings and set yourself FREE
Love to you forever
                                                    Jimi Hendrix
```

```
Diego, my love,
Remember that once you finish the fresco we will be together forever once and
for all, without arguments or anything, only to love one another.
Behave yourself and do everything that Emmy Lou tells you.
I adore you more than ever.
Your girl,
                                                    Frida
```

We get old and get used to each other. We think alike. We read each other's minds. We know what the other one wants without asking. Sometimes we irritate each other a little bit. Maybe sometimes take each other for granted. But once in a while, like today, I meditate on it and realize how lucky I am to share my life with the greatest woman I ever met. You still fascinate and inspire me. You influence me for the better. You're the object of my desire, the #1 earthly reason for my existence. I love you very much.

JC[137]

Since I left you, I have been constantly depressed. My happiness is to be near you. Incessantly I live over in my memory your caresses, your tears, your affectionate solicitude. The charms of the incomparable Josephine kindle continually a burning and a glowing flame in my heart . . . I thought that I loved you months ago, but since my separation from you I feel that I love you a thousand fold more. Each day since I knew you, have I adored you more and more.

Napoleon1[38]

Make Jam

Easy, right? Well, the tricky bit is handing it out
to your neighbors. Have you ever lamented about
the isolation of modern living and how little you
know your neighbors? Well, now's your chance to
fix it. But let's start with the easy bit. Make jam!
Pick your fruit, find the recipe, and get stirring.
While your jam is setting, give it a name and
create some homemade labels to stick on your
jars. Make your labels as colorful, poppy, and
playful as you can. Now for the tricky bit! Hit your
street and dish out your wondrous creation.
If it feels daunting, just imagine how you'd
react if someone delivered jam to your door.
Delightfully surprised or something of that ilk,
no doubt. Good, now get jamming!

The jam-drop taught me...

It Could Be Worse

Perhaps the ultimate in the It Could Be Worse series . . . Imagine if you were on the drama and the disaster that is *The Bachelor*. Yes, that train wreck of a TV show where one lucky guy dates twenty girls at the same time. It's polygamy in disguise, and no matter how we try, we just can't look away. We've all seen it. We've all cringed. We've all wished it would just stop. But if you really want to feel better about things, imagine, just for a second, that you were a contestant on *The Bachelor*. Here's how it would look.

- You step out of a limo (that part isn't so shabby) and are expected to have a quick, clever one-liner ready to go about your "first impression" of this guy.

- Your first date of the evening is his twentieth date of the evening.

- If you do decide to make out, you don't just get sloppy seconds, you get sloppy twenty-seconds.

- You have to pretend to hate all the other girls.

- You have to wear a cocktail dress everywhere you go.

- After days of drinking, all you want is water, but every time you ask for it, you are given more vodka.

- You have to endure all-nighters every day of the week on a running total of three hours' sleep.

- You have to go on "group dates" which invariably include obscure sports, embarrassing pursuits, or terrifying activities.

- Your encouragement to keep up the humil-
iation is a $2 rose. Not a plane ticket to Rome,
not a pair of Manolos, not even a movie ticket.
At the very least, they better trim the thorns
off those suckers.

- Your chances of drunk-crying are inevitable.

- Your chances of sober-crying are inevitable.

- Your only friends for weeks (or months) are
girls you just met, who are dating the same
guy as you.

- Your likelihood of having your favorite dress
torched or torn is high.

- An entire nation judges your flirt and chat
techniques.

- You have to re-watch your own antics long
after you've been sent home, and then talk
about them again on a catch-up show months
later, by which point you want to just forget
the whole thing ever happened.

ALL DONE!

Here's to you! You've walloped an impressive forty-eight challenges and filled up on all sorts of ridiculous trivia, trifles, and nonsense along the way. With a little luck, this book has reconnected you to some old passions, penchants, and pals and unearthed new ones too. You may not be exactly where you want to be yet, but take yourself back to how you felt when you first opened the book and when you took on your first challenge. No doubt you've evolved in some pretty epic ways. Progress an be hard to identify when you're in the thick of it, so show yourself some love and pop that champagne!

Rather than slip back to normality, take completing this book as an opportunity to commit to continue your fearless and adventurous quest, and create some challenges of your own. Dream up five profound, personal, and peculiar things you want to slay over the next six months. Perhaps it's something you've always dreamed of doing, or an idea of yours that keeps calling, or even exploring a new interest that's freshly piqued. This is your final challenge. You've got this.

1.

2.

3.

4.

5.

ANSWERS

Get Styled (fill in the blanks)

1. language   2. concentrate   3. Simplicity   4. knowing   5. imprisonment
6. men   7. intriguing   8. dress   9. Elegance   10. Fashions   11. shoes

Get Creative (riddle me this)

1. Pablo Picasso   2. Salvador Dali   3. Dr. Seuss   4. Amy Poehler   5. Gianni Versace   6. Albert Einstein
7. Lena Dunham   8. Vincent Van Gogh   9. Steve Jobs   10. Maya Angelou

Halfway Mark Pop Quiz

1.   c) 3
2.   b) False (they actually have five pseudo-hearts (that's a heart with one chamber, not four)
3.   b) Zebrafish
4.   a) Cheetah
5.   a) Hummingbird
6.   a) True
7.   c) 3 (and fish have two)
8.   a) True
9.   a) Giraffe
10.   b) Mini Cooper

Get Exploring (odd exploration game)

Answers: Unbelievably, they are all true.

Get Generous (give it away now!)

1. Myanmar   2. United States.   3. New Zealand.   4. Canada   5. Australia
6. United Kingdom   7. Netherlands   8. Sri Lanka   9. Ireland   10. Malaysia[139]

NOTES

1   http://www.medicaldaily.com/science-breaking-how-heartbreak-hurts-your-physical-and-mental-health-306320

2   https://www.google.com/webhp?sourceid=chrome-instant&ion=1&espv=2&ie=UTF-8#q=science%20of%20getting%20rid%20of%20emotional%20items

3   http://articles.latimes.com/2014/mar/21/health/la-he-keeping-stuff-20140322

4   http://blogs.wsj.com/economics/2011/04/23/number-of-the-week-americans-buy-more-stuff-they-dont-need/

5   http://www.dailymail.co.uk/news/article-2117987/Lost-today-Misplaced-items-cost-minutes-day.html

6   http://www.telegraph.co.uk/foodanddrink/healthyeating/10563419/The-10-weirdest-fad-diets-in-history.html?frame=endScreen

7   http://www.cosmopolitan.com/health-fitness/advice/a35415/craziest-diets-ever-debunked/

8   http://www.shape.com/weight-loss/tips-plans/9-international-fad-diets-too-wacky-believe

9   NAPO: http://www.restassuredpros.com/organizing/

10 http://www.berkeleywellness.com/self-care/preventive-care/slideshow/8-fascinating-facts-about-tears

11 https://www.phactual.com/17-facts-about-crying-tears-you-may-not-have-known/

12 http://www.berkeleywellness.com/self-care/preventive-care/slideshow/8-fascinating-facts-about-tears

13 http://www.berkeleywellness.com/self-care/preventive-care/slideshow/8-fascinating-facts-about-tears

14 http://www.berkeleywellness.com/self-care/preventive-care/slideshow/8-fascinating-facts-about-tears

15 http://phenomena.nationalgeographic.com/2013/10/07/why-a-little-mammal-has-so-much-sex-that-it-disintegrates/

16 https://www.buzzfeed.com/kellyoakes/so-many-penis-spines?utm_term=.oyAkQbZOQw#.bozAYVqzYK

17 http://theweek.com/articles/550686/22-weird-facts-about-animal-sex

18 http://theweek.com/articles/550686/22-weird-facts-about-animal-sex

19 http://www.mayoclinic.org/healthy-lifestyle/stress-management/in-depth/stress-relief/art-20044456?pg=1

20 http://www.mayoclinic.org/healthy-lifestyle/stress-management/in-depth/stress-relief/art-20044456?pg=1

21 http://www.mayoclinic.org/healthy-lifestyle/stress-management/in-depth/stress-relief/art-20044456?pg=1

22 http://www.mayoclinic.org/healthy-lifestyle/stress-management/in-depth/stress-relief/art-20044456?pg=1

23 http://www.tipsywriter.com/blog/15-interesting-facts-laughing/

24 http://www.tipsywriter.com/blog/15-interesting-facts-laughing/

25 http://www.biography.com/news/amy-poehler-quote

26 http://www.tipsywriter.com/blog/15-interesting-facts-laughing/

27 http://www.tipsywriter.com/blog/15-interesting-facts-laughing/

28 http://www.theatlantic.com/technology/archive/2012/12/55555-or-how-to-laugh-online-in-other-languages/266175/

29 http://metro.co.uk/2016/01/02/how-people-type-laughter-around-the-world-5596241/

30 http://metro.co.uk/2016/01/02/how-people-type-laughter-around-the-world-5596241/

31 http://indy100.independent.co.uk/article/these-are-10-of-the-worst-mistakes-in-history--e1xiqTmG61W

32 http://indy100.independent.co.uk/article/these-are-10-of-the-worst-mistakes-in-history--e1xiqTmG61W

33 http://list25.com/25-biggest-and-most-embarrassing-mistakes-ever-made/2/

34 http://www.forbes.com/sites/erikaandersen/2013/10/04/it-seemed-like-a-good-idea-at-the-time-7-of-the-worst-business-decisions-ever-made/#1eb36140230b

35 http://www.forbes.com/sites/erikaandersen/2013/10/04/it-seemed-like-a-good-idea-at-the-time-7-of-the-worst-business-decisions-ever-made/#1eb36140230b

36 https://www.theguardian.com/uk/2011/mar/30/washing-lions-tower-london

37 https://www.theguardian.com/culture/gallery/2012/apr/01/10-best-april-fool-hoaxes

38 http://news.nationalgeographic.com/2015/03/150331-april-fools-day-hoax-prank-history-holiday/

39 http://www.mirror.co.uk/news/weird-news/april-fools-day-top-10-1788823

40 http://www.theweek.co.uk/57930/april-fools-day-best-pranks-of-2016-and-of-all-time

41 http://www.theweek.co.uk/57930/april-fools-day-best-pranks-of-2016-and-of-all-time

42 http://priceonomics.com/when-taco-bell-bought-the-liberty-bell/

43 http://www.theweek.co.uk/57930/april-fools-day-best-pranks-of-2016-and-of-all-time

44 http://www.mirror.co.uk/news/weird-news/april-fools-day-top-10-1788823

45 http://www.huffingtonpost.co.uk/karen-pine/fashion-psychology_b_5650424.html

46 http://www.alux.com/elton-johns-crazy-glasses-collection/

47 http://listverse.com/2012/12/24/10-fascinating-facts-about-color/

48 http://www.everythingaudrey.com/35-audrey-hepburn-facts/

49 http://www.audrey1.org/biography/16/audrey-hepburn-timeline-1929-1949

50 http://www.everythingaudrey.com/35-audrey-hepburn-facts/

51 http://mashable.com/2014/08/28/antiques-roadshow-valuable-items/ http://www.therichest.com/luxury/most-expensive/the-10-most-expensive-finds-on-antiques-roadshow/

52 http://creatingminds.org/articles/age.htm http://www.huffingtonpost.com/james-clear/make-more-art-the-health-benefits-of-creativity_b_8868802.html

53 http://www.self.com/flash/fitness-blog/2014/09/infographic-pretty-cool-facts-exercise-happiness/

54 http://vkool.com/facts-about-exercise/

55 https://www.benenden.co.uk/100yrsfitness/index.html

56 https://www.buzzfeed.com/jeremybender/unbelievably-ridiculous-world-sports?utm_term=.qt40J6vOJp#.jeL6ZO7gZX

57 http://www.roughguides.com/article/the-worlds-strangest-sports/

58 http://www.telegraph.co.uk/culture/music/music-news/11495623/biggest-bands-splitting-up.html

59 http://www.telegraph.co.uk/culture/music/music-news/11495623/biggest-bands-splitting-up.html

60 http://www.rollingstone.com/music/lists/valentines-day-special-the-10-messiest-band-breakups-20130214/oasis-19691231

61 http://www.dailymail.co.uk/news/article-3548557/The-real-story-Guns-N-Roses-reunion-Duff-McKagan-brokered-multi-million-dollar-deal-Axl-Slash-split-controlling-wife.html

62 http://mashable.com/2015/03/25/band-breakups-music-history/#Y_h74hWvKiqG

63 http://mashable.com/2015/03/25/band-breakups-music-history/#Y_h74hWvKiqG

64 http://www.space.com/29940-stephen-hawking-new-horizons-pluto-flyby.html

65 http://www.scientificamerican.com/article/curiosity-prepares-the-brain-for-better-learning/

66 http://www.kickassfacts.com/25-kickass-and-interesting-facts-about-explorers/

67 http://www.kickassfacts.com/25-kickass-and-interesting-facts-about-explorers/

68   http://www.kickassfacts.com/25-kickass-and-interesting-facts-about-explorers/

69   http://list25.com/25-interesting-facts-about-explorers-and-exploration-you-might-not-know/

70   http://list25.com/25-interesting-facts-about-explorers-and-exploration-you-might-not-know/

71   http://list25.com/25-interesting-facts-about-explorers-and-exploration-you-might-not-know/3/

72   http://list25.com/25-interesting-facts-about-explorers-and-exploration-you-might-not-know/4/

73   https://neuron.illinois.edu/files/U3_L1_Supplement_Caveman.pdf

74   http://list25.com/25-interesting-facts-about-explorers-and-exploration-you-might-not-know/4/

75   http://list25.com/25-interesting-facts-about-explorers-and-exploration-you-might-not-know/4/

76   http://www.brainyquote.com/quotes/quotes/r/renzopiano404359.html

77   http://www.cnbc.com/2014/12/29/The-worlds-most-expensive-divorce-settlements.html?slide=6

78   http://www.express.co.uk/celebrity-news/331195/Top-15-cataclysmic-celebrity-divorces-to-rival-Tom-Cruise-and-Katie-Holmes

79   http://www.cnbc.com/2014/12/29/The-worlds-most-expensive-divorce-settlements.html?slide=9

80   https://www.accesshollywood.com/galleries/top-10-most-expensive-celebrity-divorces-1661/#5

81   http://www.independent.ie/style/celebrity/celebrity-features/10-most-explosive-things-weve-learned-about-heather-mills-since-divorcing-paul-mccartney-34653570.html

82   http://www.cnbc.com/2014/12/29/The-worlds-most-expensive-divorce-settlements.html?slide=9

83   http://www.today.com/id/24712537/ns/today-today_entertainment/t/order-court-messiest-celebrity-divorces/#.V2mBn2QrLx4

84   http://www.dailymail.co.uk/tvshowbiz/article-1078782/It-money-Guy-Ritchie-just-10million-Madonna-divorce-settlement.html

85   http://www.eonline.com/news/340716/katie-holmes-got-how-much-from-tom-cruise-in-divorce-deal

86   https://www.psychologytoday.com/blog/feeling-it/201208/connect-thrive

87   https://www.psychologytoday.com/blog/feeling-it/201208/connect-thrive

88   https://www.psychologytoday.com/blog/feeling-it/201208/connect-thrive

89   https://www.psychologytoday.com/blog/the-athletes-way/201402/maintaining-healthy-social-connections-improves-well-being

90   http://www.webmd.com/hypertension-high-blood-pressure/features/6-ways-pets-improve-your-health

91   http://www.creativedisplaysnow.com/articles/history-of-communication-from-cave-drawings-to-the-web/

92   http://www.skwirk.com/p-c_s-11_u-26_t-70_c-247/nsw/science-technology/way-out-communication/delivering-messages/early-methods

93   http://www.historyofinformation.com/expanded.php?id=162

94   http://thehistoryofmedia.weebly.com/smoke-signals.html

95   http://www.skwirk.com/p-c_s-11_u-26_t-70_c-247/nsw/science-technology/way-out-communication/delivering-messages/early-methods

96   https://chudbeagleblog.wordpress.com/2013/09/04/100-pitiful-album-titles-to-laugh-at/

97   http://www.independent.co.uk/life-style/food-and-drink/features/aphrodisiacs-10-best-foods-to-get-you-in-the-mood-10043642.html

98   http://www.brainyquote.com/quotes/keywords/oyster.html

99   http://www.independent.co.uk/life-style/food-and-drink/features/aphrodisiacs-10-best-foods-to-get-you-in-the-mood-10043642.html

100   http://www.independent.co.uk/life-style/food-and-drink/features/aphrodisiacs-10-best-foods-to-get-you-in-the-mood-10043642.html

101   http://www.napatrufflefestival.com/truffles-the-aphrodisiac-science-and-lore/

102   http://www.independent.co.uk/life-style/food-and-drink/features/aphrodisiacs-10-best-foods-to-get-you-in-the-mood-10043642.html

103   https://encyclopaediaoftrivia.blogspot.com/2011/12/avocado.html

104   http://www.cosmopolitan.com/sex-love/advice/g1022/aphrodisiac-foods-0509/?slide=2

105   http://www.delish.com/food/g2112/food-aphrodisiacs/?slide=9

106   http://www.independent.co.uk/life-style/food-and-drink/features/aphrodisiacs-10-best-foods-to-get-you-in-the-mood-10043642.html

107   http://www.independent.co.uk/life-style/food-and-drink/features/aphrodisiacs-10-best-foods-to-get-you-in-the-mood-10043642.html

108   http://www.nydailynews.com/life-style/weird-fetishes-exist-article-1.2436730

109   http://www.nydailynews.com/life-style/weird-fetishes-exist-article-1.2436730

110   http://www.nydailynews.com/life-style/weird-fetishes-exist-article-1.2436730

111   http://www.huffingtonpost.com/2013/10/23/sexual-fetish_n_4144418.html

112   http://www.nydailynews.com/life-style/weird-fetishes-exist-article-1.2436730

113   http://www.nydailynews.com/life-style/weird-fetishes-exist-article-1.2436730

114   http://www.nydailynews.com/life-style/weird-fetishes-exist-article-1.2436730

115   http://metro.co.uk/2015/12/27/violet-fenn-13-most-unusual-fetishes-5487670/

116   http://metro.co.uk/2015/12/27/violet-fenn-13-most-unusual-fetishes-5487670/

117   http://metro.co.uk/2015/12/27/violet-fenn-13-most-unusual-fetishes-5487670/

118   http://metro.co.uk/2015/12/27/violet-fenn-13-most-unusual-fetishes-5487670/

119   http://www.cosmopolitan.com/sex-love/advice/g3021/fetishes/?slide=4

120   http://www.huffingtonpost.com/2013/10/23/sexual-fetish_n_4144418.html

121   http://www.thedatereport.com/dating/sex/sexual-fetishes-emetophilia-tree-sex/

122   http://www.brainyquote.com/quotes/quotes/w/winstonchu131192.html

123   http://www.happify.com/hd/science-of-giving-infographic/

124   http://www.chicagotribune.com/lifestyles/health/sc-hlth-0812-joy-of-giving-20150806-story.html

125   http://www.happify.com/hd/science-of-giving-infographic/

126   http://www.online-phd-programs.org/bizarre-research-paper-topics/

127   http://www.huffingtonpost.com/2013/09/23/worlds-largest-cheesecake_n_3975141.html

128   http://www.guinnessworldrecords.com/world-records/longest-sandwich

129   http://www.guinnessworldrecords.com/world-records/largest-lasagna-lasagne

130   http://www.telegraph.co.uk/foodanddrink/foodanddrinkpicturegalleries/9792750/20-astonishing-Guinness-World-food-records.html?frame=2448061

131   http://www.dailymail.co.uk/femail/article-2770717/World-s-expensive-cocktail-goes-sale-nearly-9-000-Flute-contains-vintage-Cristal-rare-liquid-gold-Armagnac.html

132   http://www.guinnessworldrecords.com/world-records/most-champagne-bottles-sabered-simultaneously-

133   http://www.telegraph.co.uk/foodanddrink/foodanddrinkpicturegalleries/9792750/20-astonishing-Guinness-World-food-records.html?frame=2448054

134   https://www.ncdps.gov/DPS-Services/Crime-Prevention/Litter-Free-NC/Litter-Facts

135   http://www.goodreads.com/quotes/63417-you-re-always-with-yourself-so-you-might-as-well-enjoy

136   http://www.fastcodesign.com/1669022/12-hand-written-love-letters-from-famous-people-from-henry-viii-to-michael-jordan

137   https://www.buzzfeed.com/maitlandquitmeyer/15-famous-love-letters-that-will-make-you-a-romantic?utm_term=.nepN3zx53Z#.gg6ZRpolRX

138   https://www.buzzfeed.com/maitlandquitmeyer/15-famous-love-letters-that-will-make-you-a-romantic?utm_term=.nepN3zx53Z#.gg6ZRpolRX

139   http://www.npr.org/sections/goatsandsoda/2015/11/28/457101304/youll-never-guess-the-most-charitable-nation-in-the-world

Acknowledgments

To Mum, Dad, Gemma, and Milli for being the best family on the planet and supporting all my ideas (good and bad). To the one and only Hema Patel for making this book look so pretty I could cry and for all the garage jams. To Ollie for being the ultimate partner in crime (and for letting this book come on our road trip). To my amazing team for their endless energy and dedication, especially Cassie Cioproyana and her killer wit, Brianna Porter for her fearless feminism and Daniella Appolonia for her scientific sleuthing. To Fran and Doyin for their guidance in making this happen. To my amazing girlfriends for being such an inspiring force of bad-assery . . . Alex, Taryn, Samara, Vic, Kate, Sars, Josette, Cara, Chido, Sophie, Lizanne, Lesley, Bree, Linda, Bea, LJ , Leslie, Annie, Laura, Bess, Zsofi and Chris . . . you rock my world.